Designated
for Success

A Look at Career Strategies for Insurance Professionals . . .

- ■ Winning Strategies

- ■ Losing Strategies

- ■ How to Recover from Job Loss or Career Sidetracks and

- ■ Winning Everything in the End

by Donald J. Hurzeler, CPCU, CLU

Published by the CPCU Society
720 Providence Road
Malvern, PA 19355
(800) 932-CPCU
www.cpcusociety.org

ISBN 0-9760833-0-2

Designated *for Success*

■ Dedication

I dedicate this book to my parents, Jim and Coleen Hurzeler. My dad taught me to never give up. My mom believes in me always. Together, they gave me the freedom to make my own mistakes and to build the kind of confidence I would need to accomplish my goals in life. The love we have for one another is forever. I am a very appreciative son.

Although this book is dedicated to my parents, my life is dedicated to my family. I stand for the success of my wonderful wife, Linda, and our two grown children, Jim Hurzeler and Stephanie Stanczak. You have made my life complete. I love you with all my heart.

Designated *for Success*

■ Acknowledgements

I t is kind of odd that something as potentially devastating as cancer can actually cause something good to happen in one's life. That is how it worked for me. Having and recovering from cancer caused me to get off my ever-increasing large posterior and write this book. So, although I am not in the mood to acknowledge the cancer, I do want to acknowledge those in the chain of turning that experience into something positive.

At the beginning of the chain is Loretta Malandro, Ph.D. I sought her coaching around the subject of why I couldn't manage to find the focus to get a book written. She gave me the coaching I needed (I think she said something along the lines of "Just do it") and, by gosh, I did it. Thank you, Loretta!

Next in the chain was my old friend Bob Gorman. Bob is a professional writer. He had listened to me speak over the years and encouraged me to write my book. More importantly, he agreed to do a first edit of the manuscript. And edit he did.

Turns out I must have slept through some of the grammar lessons in school. Thankfully, Bob stayed awake. He cleaned up the grammar, corrected the spelling, and had the strength to tell me what needed improved and what needed removed. I listened to him and worked as hard on draft two as I had on draft one. Thank you, Bob!

And now the challenge of finding a publisher. A big thank you to the numerous people who hooked me up with their contacts. Finding a publisher for a first book is a bigger challenge than writing the book.

Along the way, I met Mac Anderson. Mac is the founder of Successories, an author, and an outstanding speaker. He was extremely generous with his time and advice. I very much appreciate his input. Thank you, Mac!

Which leads me to Jim Marks, CAE, CPCU, AIM. Jim is the executive vice president of the CPCU Society. He read my manuscript and came up with an idea. Why not take my book that covered careers in general and make it more specific to the careers of insurance professionals? He also proposed that the CPCU Society publish the book. Bingo . . . I had a publisher. Thank you, Jim!

The CPCU Society staff has done all the rest of the work. Deborah Vondran began the editing process and was a creative inspiration. Pi-Lan Hsu was charged with completing the project and has been a terrific partner. Joan Satchell designed and formatted the book, and her creativity is reflected throughout it. And Michele Ianetti has pretty much done all the publishing work. I want to thank Deborah and Pi-Lan and give special thanks to Michele and Joan for all of their excellent work. Thank you all.

I want to give a special acknowledgement to all those who hold the CPCU designation. Thank you for giving me the opportunity to live out my dreams. I am proud to be a CPCU.

■ Table of Contents

Designated *for Success*

Designated *for Success*

■ Introduction

Each time I have an opportunity to talk to a group about their careers in the insurance industry, I ask for a show of hands. "How many of you have changed jobs in the last three years?" One-third or more of the people in the audience raise their hands. "How many of you suspect you may need to change jobs in the next three years?" Most of the rest raise their hands. "I suspect that the rest of you are sitting next to your boss and cannot really put your hand up right now." Nervous laughter.

We are an industry in the midst of change. Some industries changed overnight. American steel workers were employed one day and unemployed the next. Bank tellers couldn't be hired fast enough one day and were no longer needed the day after the introduction of the ATM. Our industry is changing much more slowly.

When I started out in the business, the competition consisted of the big and little Aetna, Continental, USF&G, Kemper, Reliance, INA, and The Home. We dealt with brokers like Fred S. James, Johnson & Higgins, Alexander & Alexander, and Sedgwick. If we had a question regarding an agency we called on the Professional Insurance Agents (PIA) or the Independent Insurance Agents of America (IIAA).

Over the years all of the above companies, brokers, and institutions have changed. Some have merged. Some have been bought out. Others have gone out of business. With hundreds and thousands of separate entities in our business, the changes we are experiencing will continue for the rest of our careers.

So, are you ready for the change ahead? This book is about your career as an insurance professional. I wrote it in five parts:

■ **Winning Career Strategies** . . . the common traits I have observed in those who end up fulfilling their career dreams.

■ **Losing Career Strategies** . . . the common mistakes that insurance professionals make that keep them struggling.

■ **How to Recover** . . . a game plan for getting back on track should you hit a plateau, run into a glass or reinforced concrete ceiling, or just plain lose your job.

■ **Winning Everything in the End** . . . some thoughts on the "self-actualization" end of Maslov's Hierarchy of Need.

■ **Words of Encouragement** . . . how to be a winner in waiting.

Stuff happens in an insurance career. It is up to you to steer those events that are often out of your control, back onto a path that will take you to whatever success you desire. This book is about taking charge of your own career. It is about being the CEO in charge of your career.

And this book is designed to encourage you to reconnect with your dreams. Once you have made that connection, I know that you can make your dreams come true.

"Life is a collection of self-fulfilling prophecies."

—John Nabor

Designated *for Success*

Part One—
How to Win

"Reach beyond your grasp. Your goals should be grand enough to get the best of you."

—Teilhard De Chardin

Designated *for Success*

■ Chapter 1
Set Goals Big Enough to Hold a Lifetime of Work

"For supreme happiness, a man has to reach one of his grand goals."

—President Gerald Ford

E
ventually, I ask everyone who works for me this question: "What do you want to do with your life? I am not interested in what reality or your present circumstances tell you that you can accomplish with your life. I am not interested in what your mom or dad wants you to do . . . what your spouse wants you to do . . . what your friends expect you to do. I want to know what you really, honestly, wish and want . . . down to your bone marrow . . . dream about just before you go to sleep . . . what is it **you** want to accomplish with your one and only life?"

The answer I get most often is, "I have no idea."

Pretty disappointing to hear.

The second most common response is, "I want your job."

Now that is really disappointing. I am never perfectly happy with my job. And most people who say they want my job are just about my age and really only a step or two away from getting my job. What about the 10 or 20 years left in their working careers? What do they want to do with those decades?

Really Big Goals

In high school I ran track and had, in my eyes, one of the greatest coaches ever. Coach Bill O'Rourke introduced me to the idea of not just making the track team. He got me thinking about becoming an Olympic champion. From the very first time I met him, he began to convince me that I would eventually win the Olympic gold medal.

At first, I thought he was out of his mind. I dared not even mention his crazy notion to anyone else. Anyone I mentioned this nutty notion to would surely laugh right in my face. High school was tough enough. I didn't need people lining up to laugh at my dreams.

But, funny thing, the idea of winning the Olympic gold **did** become my dream. Coach O'Rourke made the idea come alive for me. He made sure I got to see Olympic athletes compete in person. He compared my progress to theirs. He introduced me to a couple of Olympians. I quickly saw that they were just human beings. At some point I went from praying to earn an athletic letter for track to getting anxious for my success to catch up with my desire. No doubt about it, I was going to win Olympic gold.

I ran track for 10 years. I never did win that Olympic gold medal. Didn't come close. But I did learn a few things from the experience. I learned to dream big.

Dream Big

"If we did all the things we are capable of doing, we would literally astonish ourselves."

—Thomas Alva Edison

We human beings have a hard time creating huge goals for ourselves. We just cannot imagine what is actually possible from a lifetime of work. It is very difficult to imagine what can be done in 40, 50, or more years of achievement.

The truth is that it is almost always more than we ever dreamed.

Designated *for Success*

You can look at my dream of becoming an Olympic champion and feel sorry for me that I failed to reach my goal. But save your pity. That goal moved me forward like no other goal I had set before in my young life. It gave me direction, a standard to measure against, something to look forward to for all my hard work. And, it allowed me to accomplish much more with my athletic career than I had any reasonable reason to expect. Most importantly, it taught me to set huge goals—goals that would take a lifetime to meet. How big and compelling are the goals you've set for yourself?

My uncle Pat McDonald also contributed to my ability to set goals. He introduced me to the concept of seeking to be in the top 1 percent of everything I do. Now there is a big goal! Work hard enough to move ahead of 99 percent of your fellow human beings at any particular endeavor.

The idea of setting a goal of being in the top 1 percent of anything you really want to accomplish in your life turns out to be pretty sound. In fact, it fit right in with my Olympic dreams, as well. I may not have ended up with the gold I sought, but I probably did end up in the top 1 percent of athletes in my event. And it turns out that there are rewards in the top 1 percent.

Life is not fair and equal. Being in the top 1 percent of just about anything gives you the lion's share of recognition, satisfaction, and compensation. And, the compensation is way beyond those in the remaining 99 percent. The closer to the top, the more the difference in compensation (and all the things that go with it). If you are the third highest person in your company, you probably already know that your boss doesn't earn just 5 percent more than you. She or he earns multiple times more than you. And the top dog—well, it is downright amazing how much more that person makes. Life ain't fair, and the top 1 percent are the ones that benefit from that axiom.

Be Specific but Directional

It is probably not a good idea to set a goal as a 21-year old just out of college that says, "I want to be the chairman of AIG." Better to set a specific but directional goal that says something like "I want to run an insurance company." Rule of thumb: if it's a goal you can realistically reach in 10 years, you have very much underestimated what you can really accomplish with a lifetime of work. Think big. Think specific, but directional. Give yourself some flexibility.

Some goals can be reached inside 10 years. For example, becoming a doctor. That is a great goal, as far as it goes. But I would urge you to think in terms of "I want to become the leading heart surgeon in the world," or "I want to find the cure for cancer." And since I have had a bit of cancer, I hope a whole bunch of you go after that last goal and reach it sooner rather than later.

To get specific about the insurance industry, setting an early goal to get a CPCU designation and/or a master's degree in insurance and risk management or actuarial science is an outstanding idea. It will help you on your way to achieving your lifelong goals. It will give you confidence. It is an important part of a first-class résumé. There are milestones along the way to reaching your lifelong goals. Earning an advanced degree or professional designation is an important milestone.

Great big goals will keep your interest for a lifetime. Careers are different than love. In a career, the chase may be the most interesting part. Chase a big dream. It will keep you happy for a lifetime.

Share Your Dreams

My wife Linda decided to run a marathon when she was almost 50 years of age. She had never run more than six miles at a time in her whole life. She had only six weeks to prepare for the race. It was snowing where we lived, so she had to do every mile of training indoors on a treadmill. Since I had run a bunch of marathons, she asked me to coach her. I agreed.

My first bit of coaching was for her to get a full physical and a doctor's permission. She did. Next, we agreed on a work plan to get her ready. Then I asked her to choose her five best friends, some neighbors, a couple of people at work, along with our children and her parents. I wanted her to tell each of them that she was going to run this specific marathon and finish it without injury. She balked!

People are afraid to share their dreams. A little introspection here . . . are you comfortable sharing your dreams? Have you shared your dreams?

Saying out loud to people who are important to you that you intend to become an Olympic champion, before you have even made the varsity team . . . well, it is intimidating. They might laugh at you. They might think you are full of yourself. They might think you are nuts. They might see you as competition and start to work against you. It is scary to declare your dreams out loud. It is also extremely important that you do so.

Linda eventually did manage to tell people about her goal. Some of them actually laughed right in her face. Another person told her that she was afraid the race would kill her. Still another planted the happy thought that it was likely that her uterus would drop out during the race. (I swear this is true!) So, given this fairly typical and demoralizing response, why am I urging you to declare your dreams and goals out loud?

Declaring your goals out loud commits you to those goals. It's like backing yourself into a corner. Now you have to do it!

Accomplishing anything great takes time and tenacity. You have to move forward with people talking behind your back. Naysayers will tell you to your face that your dreams are ridiculous. That's just the way it works. Learn to ignore those who spit on your dreams. They have seriously underestimated you.

If you learn nothing else out of this book, **learn to become the kind of person that embraces the dreams of others.** The world is in short supply of those who can listen to an outrageously large goal or dream and say to that person, "You can do it. How can I help you?"

And, as the person in charge of your own career, the only person who has to believe in your dreams turns out to be you.

By the way, Linda not only told her friends and relatives that she was going to finish the Las Vegas Marathon, she actually did it! She is now a marathoner forever.

Linda proved it. Big dreams and a powerful commitment can drag you at least 26.2 miles in the desert heat.

In the insurance business, the CEO creates the vision for the future. In a very real sense, you are the CEO of your career. Your dream is your vision. It is the magnet that will pull you in the direction you want to go throughout your career. Dream big.

"When you determined what you want, you have made the most important decision in your life. You have to know what you want in order to attain it."

—Douglas Lurtan

■ Chapter 2
How Will You Compete?

"*Actually, all I ever wanted to be was the best in my field.*"

—Lou Holtz

S o, if you want to be the best in your chosen part of the insurance industry, how are you going to do it? That's the second question I end up asking virtually everyone who works for me. And here are the related questions.

On what basis are you going to compete? How are you going to attain your goals? What makes you special?

And the answers I get . . . phew! Most people have never given these questions a moment's thought. In fact, I almost always have to give them some examples of what I mean.

"I will compete by being the daughter of the owner of the business."
By the way, this one is a highly effective means of competing. It does, however, require you to be extra careful in your selection of parents.

"I will work harder than anyone else."
This is a difficult strategy. It requires you to work harder than **everyone.** That is a tall order. When I was a kid, just starting off on my career, I chose this strategy. My workmates gave me a nickname of "Hustler."

I worked my fanny off. Then, along came another hard worker. He put in every hour that I put in—and more. When I kept up with him, he turned to amphetamines to keep him wired up into the night. Eventually, even I had to say that he could work harder than me. So much for my competitive advantage. And when he finally had a health crisis, so much for his competitive advantage.

"I will be smarter than everyone else."
Really? I guess you have not met that young man from McKinsey who has a Harvard M.B.A. and a doctorate from Oxford. I have met that guy and he and I are not in the same league mentally. I will bet you feel the same way when you meet him.

"I will become a technical expert on a specific subject."
Actually, this one is pretty good. It does have one problem. I set out to be *the* expert on a specific profitable niche of the insurance field. Unfortunately, over the years, that niche became highly unprofitable for the entire industry. I could have invested 20 years becoming an expert on something that basically no longer exists. Be careful.

"I will tie my star to the future chairman of the company."
I tried this one for a while. Worked great. Unfortunately, this uncaring person was rude enough to reach mandatory retirement age. When he retired, I learned that there was hell to pay. My guy was gone and my competitors had been waiting a long time to team up on me. My advantage turned into a disadvantage right after the retirement party.

"I will keep jumping jobs until I reach my goal."
It could work. It probably will not. Plays hell with your retirement planning. Kind of hard to build up a loyal group of supporters.

"I will take on every difficult job that no one else wants."
This is actually a pretty good strategy. I watched a friend of mine, Bill Walsh, do this exact thing. Every time something difficult came up, he volunteered. Every time a really nasty problem came up, he was the only person in the room with a proposed solution. Bill built an empire by taking on the unloved—unloved projects and unloved responsibilities. You have to be damn good to pull this one off. Bill did it. I have always marveled at his ability and his guts.

Designated *for Success*

"I will do what I promise to do every single time, on time, and on or under budget." This is the best strategy of all. People who actually make this strategy come alive are in short supply and end up doing very well. It is pretty hard to hold back a person who delivers the results. Easier said than done. But, in the end, you have to do this one or you will not meet your goals.

"I will prepare myself for success."
I like this one. Get an outstanding education. Earn the credentials that will lead to success. Learn by doing. This is an area where my CPCU designation has really helped me. It has given me the opportunity to do things that I would never get a chance to do at work. I prepared for my success at work by learning to become successful within a CPCU Society chapter.

My favorite is . . . **"You cannot make me give up."** You can talk bad about me, to my face or behind my back. Point out my weaknesses. Make fun of my dreams. Beat me up for my failings. And I will keep on doing everything possible to deliver the promised results so I can win in the end. Bring your thick skin with you for this one. It is not for the faint of heart.

So, what is yours? **What is your game plan for making a huge dream into a reality?**

As CEO of your career, you owe it to yourself to have a strategy and the tactics identified to turn your vision—your dream—into reality.

What will you do to make you the winner you want to be? If you cannot articulate that strategy and your tactics, you have no game plan. Without a game plan, you are just waiting around to get a lucky break or you end up taking whatever life sends your way. Either way, you are not in charge. Take charge of your career!

"A dream without a plan is probably a hallucination."

—Steven Case

■ Chapter 3
Increasing Your Odds of Success

"The successful man is one who had the chance and took it."

—Rodger Babson

I have been chasing dreams and goals for five decades. As a writer, I am a fairly observant person. So here is what I have observed as the common traits of those who work their way into the top 1 percent of whatever field in which they work.

1. **Do what you say you are going to do.**

   Aligning your words with your actions will pay dividends throughout your career. People can then count on you. They can trust you. They can invest in you. You would be amazed at how few people really do exactly what they say they are going to do.

   Do you?

   I have always struggled with the idea of **"underpromise and overdeliver."** However, I wish that whoever wrote that had also given me some major-league coaching. I have often promised too much and, while delivering more than my share, fell short of delivering everything I promised. I have worked hard to correct this major mistake. I am getting better at it. As CEO of your own career, do everything you can to avoid making the same mistake. This one is "Mission Critical."

2. Put your clients' interests above your own.

"Client" can be anyone from a customer to someone you work for or who works for you. For those rare people who can actually put their clients' interests above their own, there are many rewards. Chief among them are trust and loyalty.

The CPCU Society has an ethical requirement that is part of the professional commitment of all CPCUs. "I shall strive to ascertain and understand the needs of others and place their interests above my own" comes directly out of that commitment. Not a bad business practice for people who are in a service business . . . or any business.

3. Play fair.

I like to play hardball. I was born to bang heads and to compete as hard as I can. However, playing within the rules is just as important as playing well. We need ethical behavior now more than ever. Earn a reputation for fair play and it will grant you the opportunity to compete again and again.

4. Play for the long run.

Your job probably requires that you deliver results every quarter. Fine. But you cannot treat your career the same way. If you are looking for "fair" in the short run, you are going to have a very miserable career. People you know to be slugs will be promoted above you. Bide your time. Cheaters will win the day. **Wait.** Fools will become your boss. **Outlive them.** Your accomplishment will go unrecognized. No problem.

Long term, everything turns out to be pretty much fair. It is in the short run where things get out of whack. Forget the short run. Smile at the obvious mistakes that those above you seem to make with some regularity. Your day will come.

I remember the first time I heard about "cash flow underwriting." This is the practice of writing as much business as possible so as to keep the cash flow ahead of the losses, and to pile up assets to invest. The investment income will make up for the losses incurred through poor underwriting and inadequate pricing. Cash flow underwriting companies flourished . . . or so it seemed.

In the long run, the investment markets took a downturn, the insurance losses were greater than the combined premium, and investment income and cash flow underwriting companies were in big trouble. Playing for the long run is good for careers. It is good for a book of business. Do the basics

Designated *for Success*

right over a long period of time and things will turn out very well. Ignore the flash-in-the-pan people and companies. Play for the long run. Win everything in the end.

5. *Be confident.*
The first thing I look for in a prospective employee is confidence. I do not see it all that often. I see "arrogant" a lot. I see "scared to death" one heck of a lot. I see "just let me lurk in the background" all of the time. A truly confident person is a rare find.

You build up your confidence through attitude and success. You have to believe that you are worthy of the occasional praise that comes your way. Cherish the little and not-so-little victories you earn. Learn to accept setbacks as well as success. Either way, stay confident. People like me can smell it on you. It is a perfume that works.

A good attitude comes shining through in an interview and in all aspects of life. It is contagious. And the very best thing about attitude . . . it is entirely up to you. You can choose to have a positive attitude. It is as simple as a matter of choice. Consider this quote from Shirley MacLaine, "If I had a party to attend and didn't want to be there, I would play the part of someone who was having a lovely time." Winners have good attitudes, even when they have to play the part.

6. *Learn how our business makes money.*
Seems simple. However, many people have no idea exactly how their business makes money. Get a holistic view of whatever part of the insurance business you are in. Push yourself to understand the department next door and the jobs of those in it. Understand how one part works with the next. Learn how money comes in and how that money is spent. Learn all the factors that influence the net profit or loss of the business, from taxes to investment income, capital gains—the whole deal.

I can assure you that the people who are chosen to run businesses of any size have a very good knowledge of how that business makes money. So, if your first job is in the mail room, make it part of that job to understand how every part of the business works and how the business makes it money. And at every stage of your career, know how your part of the business contributes to the overall business success.

7. *Focus on a few big-dollar items.*
Every job has dozens or, perhaps, hundreds of aspects to it. You can spend your time working on every aspect a little or on the few that are most important a lot. I am in favor of the latter approach.

At one time I was an officer in the sales department of a huge insurance company. I will not mention which one (Allstate). I carefully observed which sales managers made it and which ones failed. What I soon learned was that those who failed were those who spent their time with their worst-performing agents. They tried to get their worst performers up to the barely acceptable range. The winning sales managers devoted all of their time to their most successful agents—the agents who really brought in the money. There's a lesson there.

Figure out what activities have the greatest return on your investment of time. Spend your time on those.

8. *Quit fixing things.*
This one goes right along with the number 7 trait. Our egos and desire for accomplishment send us off tilting at windmills. Putting our efforts behind well-running and efficient processes has a much higher return on investment than fixing things. If you find yourself spending much of your time trying to be a turnaround artist, you are missing the point. The point is to make money. I suggest you quit demonstrating your skills. Demonstrate instead, your ability to make money.

9. *Value diversity.*
Do it because it makes good business sense. Do it because you never know what kind of a team, customer base, or environment you may be working with in the future. Do it because it broadens the input for problem solving. Do it to get along well in the workplace and in society. Do it to enrich your life. Value diversity, not because it is politically correct, but because it works.

10. *Have a point of view.*
Build up a point of view about how to produce a profit in your business. At some point, start to write it down. Refine it over time. Share your ideas with others. Let them help you to sharpen the point of view. In doing so, help your co-workers align around a common point of view. Pretty soon, you will all be working together effectively. And if your point of view turns out to produce the expected levels of profit, you have just put together a portable and valuable tool. If it does not produce a profit . . . well, it is back to the

drawing boards with you. But, you are still ahead of where you would have been otherwise.

Before you get ready to leave your chosen field, think about writing a book to capture what you have learned. It would be a darn shame to take 40 to 50 years of knowledge out the door with you. Leave something behind to help others.

11. *Be willing to work the hard pile.*

My friend, Chris Moresco, introduced me to the term "hard pile." I asked him how he was doing and he said that everything he had left to do was in the hard pile. So what is in the hard pile? Getting rid of poor performers. Dropping unprofitable product lines. Starting up new ventures. Charging the right price without a discount. Telling someone the truth about his or her poor performance. Using your time to do what needs to be done instead of what you want to do. Getting rid of those last three projects that have been on your desk for six months. Hard pile things.

Few people ever have the drive or guts to take on the hard pile. Most people leave it alone. They know the hard pile is there. They choose to ignore it. People who take on the hard pile day after day and year after year, eventually take over the world. Take on the hard pile. Few can. Fewer will.

12. *Take a risk.*

I had a boss who made a whole career out of hiding in the bushes. He avoided controversy like the plague. He never weighed in on anything requiring an opinion. He stayed as far away from the hard pile as is possible. He lasted for years and years.

His game plan was to last years and years. I guess you can say he was a success. That is not the way I see it. He never progressed. He never used all of his talent. He just lasted. That does not sound like "fulfillment" to me.

The people who go to the top take risks. Watch Tiger Woods play golf. He takes huge risks. Sometimes those risks lead to disaster. More often, they lead to victory. Tiger has the confidence to accept either outcome. Okay, to be fair, he accepts the victory outcome a lot better than the defeat. But, he is not afraid to fail. And he has done so publicly many times.

Be like Tiger.

"You can't reach your goals without occasionally taking some long shots."

—Anonymous

■ Chapter 4
Do the Work

"I never did anything by accident, nor did any of my inventions come by accident; they came by work."

—Thomas Alva Edison

I figured out long ago that there were three ways for me to progress faster than those around me. They were to work with a coach or mentor, get better educated, and just plain put in more hours. All three would accelerate my growth. Most of my competitors did one or two of the three. Few did all three.

Coach/Mentor

I think that a coach or mentor is about the most valuable thing you can have in your career. I have done everything I could to hold onto every single coach that came my way. I am still in frequent touch with my high school track coach, my college track coach, and many coaches from the business world. I cherish them.

Question: "How do I get a coach to take an interest in me?" Answer: You have to ask. If you have a boss or someone up the line who has taken an interest in you, let him or her know that you are interested in his or her coaching. Encourage him or her to teach you. Encourage straight feedback on your performance. Ask questions. Do all of the above over and over again, until it becomes part of the pattern of your life.

Good coaches will share techniques and ideas with you. They will encourage you to try these new ideas. They will give you feedback on your use of these new tools.

They will send you to others in the organization or elsewhere to get you the training and experience you need to progress. They will tell you the truth even when it hurts. They will be watching for you to succeed so they can acknowledge you for your growth. How cool is that?

There is an old saying, *"We stand on the shoulders of those who went before us."* So it is with a coach. You do not have to reinvent the wheel. Let the coach advance your learning by years. Things he or she learned by long trial and error, you can learn by listening and applying.

Coaches go away if you do not make the relationship valuable for them as well. The value they seek is seeing you do well. Seeing you grow. Hearing the occasional "thank you." Hearing the occasional public recognition for their efforts. Seeing you return the favor by coaching someone else. Coaches live on through their students. It is an important calling.

Earn an Educational Advantage

I have never been able to understand how people could be in a profession for their entire working life and not get the credentials they need to give them recognition as a professional. How can an insurance professional spend 40 to 50 years in our industry and never earn a Chartered Property Casualty Underwriter (CPCU) designation? I feel the same way about accountants. How can an accountant spend 40 to 50 years as an accountant and not earn a Certified Public Accountant (CPA)? How can a life insurance producer not earn a Chartered Life Underwriter (CLU)? It just doesn't make sense to me.

If you are going to be in a specific profession for decades, why not earn the certification or designation necessary to be considered a professional? Have you? Or have you at least started the process?

I am the first to admit (before someone finds out) that I was a very poor college student. I barely graduated and I'm not proud of that fact. However, I consider a college education the price of entry in today's world. If you don't have a college degree, get one. It makes no difference if you are 21 or 71. Get one. Do it for yourself.

You can earn an associate of arts degree in two years or less, or a bachelor's degree in three years or less. The CPA or CPCU or other certification/designation can be earned along the way. A master's degree is about 18 months' work past a bachelor's degree. It makes a difference. Do it for yourself.

Designated *for Success*

Getting a degree or two is just part of the journey. To be the best, you will have to commit yourself to the concept of lifelong learning. John Wooden once said, **"It's what you learn after you know it all that counts."**

Not all learning earns you a degree or certificate. Some of it is just plain useful stuff. Like learning the Quality process. Like learning to speak in front of groups. But my most important learning opportunities have been programs on people skills—listening, straight talk, dealing with conflict, and dealing with resignation (more about that one later).

Just Plain "Put in More Hours"

Now, you need not get crazy about this one. My guess is you are already putting in more hours now than most of those around you. But do the math. If you work two hours more a day than the average person, you are going to gain experience faster by some 20 to 25 percent. I put in my extra hours in the morning. I also put in a few extra hours on the weekends. Because of this, I just plain get to see more stuff that the average 9-to-5 person. The extra work adds to my value as an employee.

Warning: you can get obsessed with working long hours. There is a point of diminishing returns. Do not work until you are too tired to do good work. Do not work until you ruin the relationships with those that are special to you. Balance counts.

"*Opportunity is missed by most people because it is dressed in overalls and looks like work.*"

—Thomas Alva Edison

■ Chapter 5
Measure Your Progress

"We're still not where we're going, but we're not where we were."

—Natash Jasefowitz

J ust because you are still employed, it does not mean you are making progress toward your goals. Being honest with yourself is sometimes the hardest kind of "honest." **Are you really making good progress toward your long-term goals?** Think about it. Are you?

Here is what I know. I know that you **must** have some measure of your progress. **You must.** If you do not have such a measure, life just happens. Life just happens at its own pace, not at a pace that you have set. And the one thing none of us can really afford to waste is time.

So, set some goals and measure against them. You may wish to have this little "progress review" with yourself or with your coach on your birthday every year. You may want to measure your progress each January 1, assuming you are not so worn out from December 31 that you can actually do some serious introspection on that day. It matters not what day you pick to do this self-measurement. It does matter that you do it and that you do it consistently over time. Better yet, do it with a coach or mentor. With or without a coach, just do it.

What will you measure against? I suggest that you measure against two kinds of personal goals. The first is a set of one-year goals that you set for yourself. What do you intend to do this year? What specific educational investment will you make in yourself this coming year? What experiences will you seek in your workplace? What experiences will you seek outside of work? *I recommend that you set three to five specific things that you absolutely intend to accomplish in the next 12 months and measure against those short-term goals.* Remember, these are not the goals that your boss has set for you (although some of the goals may be the same as the ones set for you at work); these are the goals you set for yourself to propel you forward toward your long-term goals.

The second set of personal goals are long-term milestones that you have set up for yourself. These are the milestones you need to meet if you are to eventually achieve everything you have set out to achieve. These have much longer time frames attached to them. They are, what I call, "wake up to reality" milestones. If you are not hitting these milestones, it is time to "wake up to reality" and seek coaching or find a mentor to help you get back on track.

Let us look at a quick example of both kinds of personal goals:

Example of One-Year Goals

1. Improve my education. Take two parts of CPCU and pass them.

2. Improve my networking skills. Attend five CPCU, NAIW, or RIMS events this year.

3. Begin to be seen as a leader at work. Volunteer to lead a task force or project.

4. Improve my speaking skills. Attend six Toastmaster meetings.

5. Begin to take better care of myself. Get a complete physical from my doctor.

Examples of Longer-Term Milestones

1. Become a supervisor by age 25.

2. Become a manager of supervisors by age 30.

3. Earn my CPCU by age 30.

Designated *for Success*

4. Become an officer of the local CPCU Society chapter by age 35.

5. Run a profit center by age 40.

6. Own my own business by age 45.

7. Be debt-free by age 50.

8. Be financially "bullet-proof" by age 55—able to retire tomorrow if I want to.

9. Retire at age 60.

10. Write and have at least six books published by age 65.

11. Travel to 100 countries in my lifetime.

12. Be a positive influence on my children and their children until the day I die.

If you are 21 years old, you need to set up both kinds of measurements to help you achieve everything you want to achieve in life. If you are 55 years old, you need to set up both kinds of measurements to help you achieve everything you want to achieve in life. A life without a game plan set by you just happens. With a game plan set by you, you are much more likely to get to where you want to go. Set goals and measure. And do not let your boss be the only one setting goals for your life. **You are in charge of you.**

Time frames for achievement are much different today than they were when I first started setting goals some 40 years ago. Careers follow different paths. However, if you want to think about a whole working lifetime of progress toward a goal, let me give you one way to look at it. Keep in mind that I am writing about a whole lifetime of work. It covers such a long time that it may seem daunting to you to look at a whole career this way. Here goes. . . .

Let us work your career backwards. Whatever your long-term goal is, wouldn't you want to be in that position for at least three years before you retire? By the way, when do you plan to retire? Let's say 60. So, you need to be in the position you have worked your life to achieve by the time you are 57. If you start at age 22, that gives you 35 years of preparation time. How should you use the 35 years?

Take 10 years to learn the basics. I hate the way that sounds as much as you hate reading it. However, in today's complex world, it probably does take nearly a decade to really master the basics of a complex job. You can be good in a couple of years, but mastery takes time. If you have a very narrow area of interest, perhaps you can master that area much sooner. However, if you can master it quickly, that means that lots of people can master it quickly. The real value comes from mastering something difficult. And mastering something difficult takes time.

When I first started in the insurance business, I had a crusty old boss named Eric Thorson. "Old" was probably 40 at the time. "Crusty" meant that Eric just plain told the truth. And the truth he told me was that it would take me 10 years to become a good underwriter.

I thought Eric Thorson was nuts. I thought he must have been a slow learner. In fact, I was pretty upset that he would even say such a thing. Ten years! To become a good underwriter? Did he think this was brain surgery? Ten years . . . what a bunch of hooey.

Unfortunately, Eric was about right. I had to learn each line of insurance. I had to learn how to underwrite small, medium, and large risks. I needed to learn about many different types of businesses. I needed to learn about agents and brokers and how they work. I needed to become a good communicator, marketer, and negotiator. It was probably about 10 years into my career that I had really mastered the job of "underwriter."

So, let me be your Eric. It will take you about 10 years to master your core technical skill in the insurance industry. Sorry about that. It takes 10 years.

Once you have mastered the basics of your core job, it probably takes another 10 years to learn the mechanics of the rest of the profession. If you started out learning one discipline, you will need to know how the rest of the mechanism works. This decade is usually all about general management or learning new disciplines. This is the time period where master underwriters learn the finance function or how to manage a claims operation. This is where great salesmen and women learn how to value other agencies and put together acquisition deals. These are the "branch, department, or agency manager" years.

The next decade is devoted to operating as a master technician or senior executive. A happy thought, these jobs normally pay very well. These are the "chief underwriting officer," "senior actuary," or brokerage "partner" years.

The next five years can be devoted to positioning yourself for that final step across the line to your dream position. Remember all your distaste for "politics" early on

Designated *for Success*

in your career? It is time to look around you. When you have progressed this far up the corporate ladder, the air contains trace amounts of politics. Who am I kidding, the air is politics. Politics are nothing more than doing a great job while proving yourself to be a great teammate. You can do it.

Obviously, I have not outlined a scientific process. I recognize that it is possible for a 28-year old to become the CEO. I know that not all chief underwriting officers are in their 40s or 50s. But you need some basic framework for thinking about the timing of your career. If you have the same job you had at five years into your career, by the time you are 20 years into your career, it is time to face up to the fact that you stalled. Time to bust a move. Quit (but not until you have lined up the next job). Force the issue. Make something happen.

This is another place where a coach can help you. Before you even think about it, she or he will be asking you if you are satisfied with your progress.

The main rule here is, think. Think about the progress you are making. If you are not making good progress, it's time to find another path.

Set up some specific activities that, when achieved, will move you down the path toward your lifetime goals. Give these activities a 12-month period for completion. Measure your progress at the end of those 12 months. Be a tough grader. If you are not really hitting those goals, get some help. It is important that you meet the goals that you set for yourself.

And have some longer-term milestones in place to measure against for achieving your lifetime goals. If you are not hitting the milestones, it is time to get some help. Do not ignore a lack of progress toward hitting your milestones. These are your goals. This is your life. I cannot think of anything more important than making sure you get the most out of your one and only life.

"*Hope for a miracle, but don't depend on one.*"

—Talmud

Designated *for Success*

■ Chapter 6
Give Yourself Some Options and Opportunities

"*Many do with opportunities as children do at the seashore; they fill their little hands with sand and then let the grains fall through, one by one, till all are gone.*"

—T. Jones

Y ou have all the talent in the world. You have a great attitude. You work your butt off. You have been successful at everything you have ever been asked to do. So, why aren't you more successful?

I had a great boss once—Jim Strohl. Jim taught me many things. The most important thing was "suspect yourself."

"Suspect yourself" has many applications. You can use it when the project you commissioned came in late and was completed incorrectly. Before you jump all over your loyal staff, suspect yourself. Were you clear about the due date? Were you clear about what you wanted? Did you check in from time to time to see that appropriate progress was being made? Suspect yourself.

If your career is not going according to plan, suspect yourself. It may seem like the people above you are idiots. They may appear to ignore your greatness. They may be protecting their own careers. They may be playing favorites. Maybe. More likely, **you** are the cause of your lack of progress.

Life is all about options. People sometimes cram themselves into a little narrow channel and then wonder why they are not going right to the top. I say narrow, because the channel has a bottleneck. That bottleneck may be the fact that there is only one top job, a young and strong incumbent, and 20 people competing to get that job. People fool themselves into thinking their lack of progress is temporary. Maybe it is not. Think about your options.

So what do options look like in a career?

If you have decided that you will spend your entire career within an hour's drive of your home, you had better be the favorite son or daughter of the aging owner of the firm. Nothing is more confining to a career than the firm decision not to move. Let me rant on about this poor choice for a while.

I spent the first 35 years of my life living in basically the same spot. I had all of my relatives nearby. Some were aging and needed some care from me. The kids were in schools. My favorite sports—surfing and running—were accessible nearly 365 days a year. I was healthy. I knew how to get anything I needed and how to get around town. I loved my life.

At 35, I got transferred from Southern California to Chicago. I had never seen it snow. I had been in snow, but had never seen it actually fall out of the sky. I did not even own a coat. I had no idea how to drive on snow or ice or how to dress warmly. I knew almost no one in Chicago. The kids actually knew no one at all. And, rumor had it, the surfing was really poor in the Midwest.

Why would I make such a move? First of all, my employer mentioned to me that my paycheck would now be in Chicago, as would my job. To tell the truth, I was not unhappy. I was, and still am, ambitious. I knew that I had to take a tour in the home office or in another region if I was going to advance. I wanted to go.

That said, it is almost insulting to me when I hear people say "I cannot move. I have family here." As if I do not? I promise you I care for my family and friends back home.

Yes, it is inconvenient to move. It is disruptive. It is how you grow. Do not make the mistake of never trying it. But just in case you want the list of excuses, here they are:

- ■ "If I move I will never be able to afford to move back here again. The housing costs here are skyrocketing. I will be forced to buy a smaller home if I can ever return."

- ■ "My folks are getting old and need my help."

- ■ "I have young kids and count on my folks as the baby-sitter."

- ■ "My spouse has a great job and cannot move."

- ■ "My kids are getting too old to move. Maybe after they graduate from high school."

- ■ "The new place is so expensive that I will not be able to buy a house as nice as the one I am in now."

- ■ "I have allergies and have to continue with my doctors here."

- ■ "I am about to become president of the local charity."

- ■ "I just could not be comfortable anywhere else in the world."

- ■ "I do not like the snow."

- ■ "I just could not live where there are anything less than four seasons."

- ■ "The taxes are too high in the new state."

- ■ "It is not safe for Americans to live overseas right now."

Well, you get the idea. You may think that these are your unique situations. I hear them all of the time. They are all 100 percent legitimate. But, they also are all 100 percent excuses.

In the middle of writing this book, I was recruited to take a job in Asia. My wife and I had all the same discussions you might have in the same situation. Quite frankly, the thought of moving to Asia had never occurred to either of us. Our parents are aging. We are certainly comfortable in our current home, and I actually love my current job. It turned into a personal test case for this whole chapter.

We decided that the decision should be made based on whether the proposed job took me closer to reaching my career goals than my current position. It was one of the hardest decisions we have ever made together. In the end it was the right decision. In the end, the decision was moot. The job was not right and we stayed put. However, we are both kind of proud of the fact that we did not let our current comfort get in the way of making a right decision.

I know this is one of the toughest choices that most people have to make in a lifetime. I know that I am focused on presenting the case for moving in a favorable light. However, it opens up options for you if you are willing to move. It is a very important choice. As CEO of your own career, it is one of the most important decisions you will ever make. Please give it your most thoughtful consideration.

Two thoughts . . . first, **try** moving. You can move back if you hate it. Second, unemployment is not an attractive option. You may have to move to keep a job or to become employed again.

My wife, kids, and I moved a dozen times. We moved from the beach in California, to Chicago, to Pittsburgh, to Chicago, to New York City, to Baltimore, and back to Chicago. And there are a few moves left in us. We found we loved moving. To be fair, the first few moves were more fun than the last few. Also, we had to make a deal with the kids at some point that said we would make sure they stayed put from about sixth grade through high school. We have spent a lot of money on phone calls and air travel. We have run into some tight spots with relatives getting sick and us being miles away. But we have made it work. We are much better off individually and as a family for having moved.

During the time we spent moving, I was able to expand my experience from local to national and some international. I worked in the home office and saw the field from a different perspective. I have enjoyed my greatest success and a few significant setbacks. I grew in my job and made great progress toward reaching my dreams. I am in favor of moving. Please at least give it a try. If you have already made a firm decision not to move, please reopen the discussion and consider the possibilities. It is worth another look.

Moving taught me a few things about the rest of this country. There are great places to live in the United States. Chicago could not be more different than Huntington Beach, California. However, my kids got a wonderful education in Chicago. They got involved in school programs that let them travel to foreign countries. They both enjoyed good athletic careers.

We learned to play in the snow (sparingly). We actually do enjoy the four seasons (some more than others). My golf handicap improved. We found a church we love. We found great doctors . . . and needed them. We found new friends and held onto our old ones. It has been a terrific experience. And, by the way, we made a lot more money than we would have had we stayed put. Give it a try.

Designated *for Success*

Rant over. On to another strongly held belief. "I cannot afford to leave the job I am in." This is the second-most-common excuse I hear. Just because you have worked somewhere 20 years does not mean you need to be there 20 more. Let us look at what this excuse sounds like:

- ■ "I have only six more years until I qualify for retiree medical."

- ■ "If I quit now I will not get the $50,000 of paid-up life insurance they give to retirees with 35 years of service."

- ■ "I have not maxed out the retirement plan here. I only need one more year."

- ■ "This is family."

- ■ "I do not want to give up the security."

- ■ "I hate to say it, but I am really loyal to these folks."

Again, all good thoughts. One-hundred percent valid. Also, 100 percent excuses.

I stayed with one company for 27 years. It was probably the largest mistake I ever made. I would have stayed until they fired me had the company not decided to sell the part of the company that I loved. It was like a divorce I did not ask for.

I used all of the above quotes as my reasons for not wanting to leave. In the end, the part of the company I loved was sold out from under me. So much for security. So much for loyalty. I was pretty foolish sticking around as long as I did.

I want to be careful here. My dad spent 37 years with one firm. I mentioned that I spent 27. There are good and great things about being with one firm that long. My only point here is that you limit your possibilities if you do not consider all the options . . . including the option to leave one firm for another. You limit yourself. Options are important. Consider them carefully.

And a few words about the money side of making a move after you have been somewhere for a long time. New employers understand your situation. If they want you bad enough, they will pay you for making the move. You are in an excellent position to get a better title, equal amount of vacation, and a signing bonus big enough to pay for whatever you are giving up and more. Do not assume they will not pay these large sums of money. They will because they want you.

There are other barriers that people create for themselves, thus effectively limiting their options. Examples are:

- "I will not work for a small company."

- "I will not take a pay cut."

- "I will not work for him or her or some specific company."

- "I will not be a salesperson."

- "I will not manage people I know."

- "I do not want to be part of 'management.'"

- "I will not commute to an office that is 30 minutes farther away."

- "I won't live in New York City." This one is part of a theme that says, "I will move, but not to New York City, New Jersey, or anyplace in the South."

- "I cannot think about changing jobs during Little League season. I am the coach!"

- "I will not go back and get my college degree. My experience should be enough!"

- "No. I'll never shave my beard. It is part of who I am."

- "Yes, the tattoos on my fingers read 'B-O-R-N T-O L-O-S-E.' You got a problem with that?"

You get the idea. Again, all of these are more or less valid expressions. But, every one diminishes someone's options. They cut down the "at bats" they would otherwise enjoy. Fewer at bats equals fewer hits. None of them make it certain that you will not get that next great opportunity (except, perhaps, that last one). They do, however, make it more difficult. Cut down your options enough and you will never reach your dreams. Life is about options. Do not throw yours away.

Think of options as opportunities. Consider yours carefully.

"If Fortune calls, offer him a seat."

—Yiddish Proverb

Designated *for Success*

■ Chapter 7
Build Your Network

"When a friend is in trouble, don't annoy him by asking if there is anything you can do. Think up something appropriate and do it."

—Edgar Watson Howe

It is a rare Monday morning when I do not get a call or e-mail from someone who is looking for a job. Almost always on Monday. Almost always before 9:30 a.m.

Most of the people contacting me are friends or friends of friends. They are networking, trying to get a lead on a job. I appreciate the fact that they contact me. I will do all I can to help them.

Many of the people I hear from are in the capable hands of an outplacement service. They are all but forced to contact dozens or hundreds of acquaintances. Good for the outplacement people. They are having their clients do the right thing.

There are three types of networkers. I hear from all three. They are:

The **expert networkers** who are in contact with people from throughout the industry on a daily basis. For them, networking for a job is not much of an effort. They network all the time. They have built up meaningful relationships over years of contact.

The second kind of networker is the **shy networker.** This person networks, but only when desperate. He or she hates to network, and thinks it is kind of like begging. Outplacement workers push these people to do what needs to be done.

The third kind of networker is the **"has not got a clue networker."** Of the three, this one sometimes does more harm than good in networking.

For example, I got a call from a guy from my old company. "Don, gosh, I kind of lost track of you. I heard you were back in town. Just wanted to call to say hi. Also, do you have any jobs open? I just got word they are letting me go." That's the entire opening comment from a guy I used to work with side-by-side for years. A guy I have not heard from for seven years.

Here is what I heard as he was talking:

"Don, I know I didn't return your call when you left the company after 27 years. I know I didn't respond to the e-mail when you wrote me that you had cancer and were going in for surgery. I guess I could have come to your party when you returned to town and made CEO at your new company. But seriously Don, do you have a job for me?"

As steamed as I was with this guy, I did all I could to help him land a new job. In fact, he landed one at a place I recommended to him. I was glad to have helped a little bit. But I wish he had dropped me a note to tell me to quit looking around for him. I found out he had found a job. I found out months later—found out from someone else.

I cherish my network of friends and associates. I hope that I help them through life as much as they help me. And networks are not just for finding jobs. I use my network every day to:

■ Find people to hire.

■ Check out applicants.

■ Track down hard-to-find information.

■ Get new ideas.

■ Share my problems with them. Sometimes they have solutions.

■ Share good news.

Designated *for Success*

- Get support when I need it.

- Gather support for those in need.

- Generate business for my company.

- Run my ideas by them to get their reaction.

- To be at the leading edge of industry happenings.

- To check out rumors.

- To start rumors.

- To get me through the day.

A large network of people in your life is a huge asset. You cannot buy one at the store. You have to build it over time. You have to nurture it or it will wither and die. You have to be open to new entrants or it will get stale. You have to work it to keep it vibrant.

Sad truth: most people neglect their networks. ***How is your network doing?***

At the heart of my network are co-workers from the several companies where I have worked. I learned early on not to quit talking to someone just because he or she left the company. In fact, I learned that they became windows into the rest of the world, and, thus, very valuable network members.

Close to the heart of my network are the men and women of the Chartered Property Casualty Underwriters Society. There are almost 27,000 members. I do not know them all, but I sure know a bunch of them. These people come from throughout the insurance industry—our industry. I urge you to join and to become an active member. In the case of the CPCU Society, it has become a moving party of my friends. I say "moving" because the Annual Meeting and Seminars move from city to city.

Also included in my network are contacts from throughout the rest of our industry . . . lawyers, salesmen and women, vendors. At the outer ring of the network are some of my most valuable contacts—consultants and executive recruiters. These folks know what is going on in the industry faster than anyone else. They can solve problems for you (also for a large fee) and they can find you outstanding people to resolve staffing needs (usually for a large fee). They may also help you find a job just when you need one.

Some basic rules for networking:

1. Have a network.

2. Keep current on their whereabouts . . . keep a database of business cards and e-mail addresses.

3. Work the network. Call, e-mail, and keep in touch.

4. Do not keep in touch via those worthless forwarded e-mails I get all the time. That is not keeping in touch. It is annoying.

5. Check out the quote at the top of this section and put it into action. I am a big believer in the karma of helping others. Help others before you seek help yourself.

6. Keep your network up to date on your whereabouts, your current information, especially when you move offices or change jobs.

7. Do not be shy about asking for help. You will get more help than you ever dreamed possible.

8. Thank the people who help you.

9. Do not let people drop out of your network. If they die, save their card a respectable year or two and then throw it away.

10. Add new people to your network throughout your career.

As with most things in life, you are only as good as the people around you. Put together a strong network.

Today would be a great time to start or revitalize your network. A great way to start—make a call. Check in with an old colleague and ask him or her how he or she is doing. Bring him or her up to date on your job and the things going on in your life. Tell him or her you are happy to be back in contact and that you will stay in better touch. Give it a try. Your colleagues will be happy to hear from you.

And back to the concept of you as CEO of your career. Have you ever met a CEO that did not have a huge Rolodex® on his or her desk? If you have, it is because in this day and age that huge Rolodex is now sitting nicely in a computer or some other electronic gadget. CEOs got to be CEOs because they know people. You are a CEO. Fill up that Rolodex.

Designated *for Success*

"Real friendship is shown in times of trouble; prosperity is full of friends."

—Euripides

■ Chapter 8
Establish a Bedrock in Your Life

"No greater burden can be born by an individual than to know no one cares or understands."

—Arthur H. Stainback

Our lives have certainly become complex. My dad worked at the same place for 37 years. We never moved. My son-in-law is a young man and has already moved a couple of times and held numerous jobs. The insurance industry I am in is going through a prolonged period of change. People lose their jobs every day. They are forced to move from state to state, from discipline to discipline. They put up with periods of uncertainty and unemployment. As I said, life has certainly become complex.

In periods of uncertainty, I think it wise to look around and find some bedrock to cling to. All of us need some place we can always call home even when our home changes places from time to time. A place to go to in good times and in bad . . . for encouragement, networking, learning, and help.

The choices for this bedrock are numerous:

- ■ your church

- ■ family

- ■ a club or association that has chapters all across the country or world (like Rotary)

- fraternal/sorority organizations

- professional organizations

- a combination of the above

For me, I found a bedrock organization within my profession. That bedrock has been with me for almost 30 years now. It will be with me until I die and when I die they will note my passage to the current members. That organization is the Chartered Property Casualty Underwriters Society.

The CPCU Society has helped me build one of the best networks in the business. It keeps me current on industry trends. It furthers my education with event learning and through its symbiotic relationship with the American Institute for Chartered Property Casualty Underwriters—the degree-granting part of the CPCU experience. The Institutes continually enrich their course offerings with courses that will be helpful to me at any stage of my career.

Additionally, the Society offers things like resiliency workshops—event training to help me deal with the ups and downs of my business. It offers a place for me to post my résumé for potential employers to find me. It gives me an opportunity to build my skills as a volunteer. It gives me exposure that I could not gain in past or present jobs. It cares for me when I am at the top of my game, down in the dumps, and everywhere in between. It does not care where I live or what I am making. It is there at all times to stand for my success. The CPCU Society is the bedrock in my career.

Have you established a bedrock? If not, I encourage you to do so. Look for an organization that can see you through from beginning to end. That can serve you in every state and any country. That is accessible. That changes over time to meet your needs. That actually cares about you as a human being. Trust me on this . . . over a long career you will need a place to call your professional home. Find that place, support it, and benefit from it for the rest of your life.

"Brotherhood is the very price and condition of man's survival."

—Carlos P. Romulo

■ Chapter 9
Lessons Learned as a Volunteer Leader

Have you ever wondered why in the world people volunteer? I used to. And then one day a young guy named Dick Gund, CPCU, showed up at my door with a case of cold Heinekens under his arm. He introduced himself as the president of the Orange Empire Chapter of the CPCU Society. I did not know him from a hole in the ground. I did, however, know Heinekens. I invited him in.

Mr. Gund had heard that I had just passed my last exam of the CPCU series. He had come to my home to welcome me into the local chapter. About three six packs into the case of Heinekens, I also learned that he was in my home to recruit me as a volunteer for the chapter. I accepted. Heck, at that point there was no telling what I might have accepted.

It turned out to be one of the worst hangovers and best decisions of my life. Whatever little I have given to the CPCU Society in the way of my time and money has been repaid to me many times over in the lessons I have learned. Here are a few of the things I have learned as a volunteer leader:

1. *Recruiting volunteers can be fun.*
   Dick Gund taught me this lesson. First of all, very few people volunteer unless you ask them to do so. Secondly, very few people you ask turn you

down. Learning to ask people to volunteer teaches you courage, networking, sales skills, and the fact that you do not need to do the doggone thing yourself. And, if you include a case of beer, it can be one heck of a lot of fun.

2. *If you can manage volunteers, you can manage anyone.*
   Early on in my career I was not getting much opportunity to learn any management skills. I was handling an underwriting desk at work and managing no one. When I volunteered to head up a committee for my local CPCU Society chapter, I started to get a chance to manage people—a chance they would not give me at work. I learned to manage. I learned to manage without the carrot and stick that one often has at work. I learned to manage in a volunteer environment. It gave me the confidence to manage at work or anywhere. A very valuable lesson for anyone.

3. *You can survive failure.*
   I learned to recover from failure in the relatively safe setting of a volunteer organization. I would rather not have learned these lessons, but I did. I learned to make sure the speaker at your luncheon has the time and date right (a couple did not, leaving me in the lurch doing my hand-rabbit routine in front of a projector). I learned to make sure the hotel had the luncheon booked on the right day (one did not, leaving me to scramble at the last minute for space and meals). I learned to tell a joke in front of a large crowd, have it bomb, and survive the embarrassment. I learned I could even survive screwing up an assignment. More importantly, I learned that I could go to my fellow volunteers, tell them I had screwed up the assignment, ask for their forgiveness, and ask for their help. I got both the forgiveness and the help. Another lesson learned.

4. *"If you don't toot your own horn it often stays untooted."*
   I do not have that quotation exactly right, but I heard Bill Clinton say something like that on a recent interview show. He is right. I learned that you need to give some public recognition to those who do the hard work for your organization. If you do not do that horn tooting, it is likely that no one will. People are reluctant to praise themselves. Toot their horn when they do good work. A little positive reinforcement can go a long way.

5. *Leadership in the face of adversity takes real courage.*
   Years ago, I attended the CPCU Society Annual Meeting and Seminars in Honolulu. I was president-elect for the Orange Empire Chapter at the time. The president of the chapter was my good friend Tom Lorden, CPCU. We were to throw a celebration party for our new designees.

The morning of the party, Tom Lorden came to see me. He told me that his father had just passed away. Tom was heartbroken. We all hugged one another and shed some tears. It was a very unhappy time.

That afternoon Tom came to see me again. He had decided that the reason he had come to Honolulu was to honor our new designees and that was just what he was going to do. He asked me to keep the death of his father quiet until after the party. He then prepared for the party. When it was time for the party, Tom had a smile on his face and he acted as a terrific host.

I think I learned what true leaders do that evening. Tom has been one of my heroes since that event.

6. *Give a person a chance.*
   The good people of the CPCU Society's Orange Empire Chapter took a real chance on letting me be their leader. (I was president of that chapter in the early 1980s.) If you think about it, they actually let me practice my leadership and management skills on them. I was nowhere near perfect for the job. They gave me a chance.

   Over the years, I have seen the CPCU Society give dozens of people a chance. Some of those afforded a chance were very unlikely candidates. Their employer had never given them a chance to grow. They were not natural born managers or leaders. And to be truthful about it, some of them never did develop into great managers or leaders. However, the CPCU Society gave them a chance to find out if they wanted to manage, wanted to lead.

   Give people a chance. People who want to succeed will often surprise you. It turns out that desire, combined with a supportive environment and an opportunity, is a powerful formula for success. Another lesson learned.

7. *You can be a very effective leader if you do not care who gets the credit.*
   My friend, Tom Lorden, comes to mind again. He set the wheels in motion for our chapter to compete for recognition as the best mid-sized chapter in the country. He asked me to engineer his effort. I asked another Board member, Jim Robertson, CPCU, to put our efforts into some kind of an effective presentation. The members of the chapter did all the work needed to compete. Low and behold, we won the award.

   Tom sent me to the Annual Meeting to pick up the award. At our next regularly scheduled chapter meeting he praised the chapter members, me, and Jim Robertson for putting together the winning entry. Not once did he claim any credit for himself.

There is a lesson there. It is a lesson I see put in play far too infrequently in business.

8. *If you know where to look, you do not have to pay for a guide.*
   I love executive recruiters. I help them in any way that I can. They get people like me jobs when we need them, opportunities when we deserve them, and advice when we ask for it. They serve a huge need in knowing where the talent is and matching that talent with available jobs. That said, I rarely use executive recruiters, recruiters of any kind, ads in papers, or the Internet to find people to hire. Why? Because I know hundreds of talented people in our industry. I know them through my contacts at work and my contacts through the CPCU Society. I have saved my employers hundreds of thousands of dollars by not having to pay to find talent.

My employers have always supported my involvement in the CPCU Society. Part of the payback for that support comes from the lessons I have learned outside of the workplace. Volunteer work and volunteer leadership teaches many lessons. The biggest lesson of all is that you always seem to get back more than you put into any volunteer activity.

"The Golden Rule is of no use to you whatsoever unless you realize that it is your move."

—Dr. Frank Crane

■ Chapter 10
Be Ready to Greet Opportunity

"To think too long about doing a thing often becomes its undoing."

—Eva Young

W inners are ready to win. I live my life by the understanding that the bus may not come by this stop again. I know a lot of people who think opportunity is an unending river. They pass on the great opportunity in front of them because they just know there is a better one out there. Even worse, they do not even fully investigate all the opportunities that come their way.

If you get invited to play golf at Augusta National, do not pass on the opportunity thinking you will be asked again. A friend of mine had that opportunity. He passed. Too busy right now. "Let's do it early next year." There was no next year. The member who invited him died.

The biggest regrets I hear from people are always about passing on the opportunities that came their way.

An example: "I knew I should have taken the day off and gone fishing with my dad when he asked. How was I to know that he would die unexpectedly at age 72? I wish I had that time with him."

"I was too busy to take advantage of the stock opportunity when our company went public. Now all my buddies are retired on their profits and I am still here pounding away."

"When they asked me to start up the office in Pittsburgh I turned it down. Who knew it would grow to become the most profitable office in the history of the company? The lady who accepted their offer sure was lucky."

"I remember when Bill was in desperate need of a job. Wish I had returned his call then. How was I to know he would become chairman of this company?"

"I wish I had called Don earlier. He tells me that there is a perfect job out there for me but they are closing the application process on it today. Wish I had a résumé to fax them."

Here is how that last one actually happened. . . .

A dear friend of mine had been with a company for more than 20 years. One day his boss came in and tipped him off that he will be "rightsized" out of a job in about a week. My friend calls me. I know of a perfect job for him, but the application process closes in two hours. He has no résumé. He has a meeting to go to. Better pass on this one, he says.

Sure enough, he lost his job. And sure enough, the one job that was perfect for him went to someone else. Twelve months later he was still looking for a job.

I will **never** go a day without an up-to-date résumé with me at all times. You remove yourself from even being considered for opportunities if you do not even have a fresh résumé. If you think you do not need one, please think again. You do.

Businesses change overnight. You may be gold today, but you can be lead tomorrow. Twenty years' seniority means very little these days. That loyalty you feel for your company is not fully returned by the corporation. The Boy Scouts had it right, **"Be prepared."** Here is how:

1. Have your network up and running at all times.

2. Have an updated résumé ready at all times.

3. Listen for opportunity and take advantage of as many as you can.

Designated *for Success*

4. If you find you are getting lots of opportunities, but taking advantage of only a few, suspect yourself.

Taking advantage of opportunities is not easy. It requires work. It may require some sacrifice. It may require you to reciprocate somewhere down the line. You may have to get some advice.

But, the rewards are great. Lifelong memories. Strengthened relationships. New experiences. Financial rewards. No regrets. And, the possibility that the opportunity you act on may move you closer to meeting you lifelong goals.

Do not treat opportunity like an intruder. Greet it like a friend.

"And all that you are sorry for is what you haven't done."

—Margaret Widdemer

■ Chapter 11
Never Give Up

"Never grow a wishbone, daughter, where your backbone ought to be."

—Clementine Paddleford

People give up or get discouraged. It is a fact. Has it ever happened to you? Later on I will spend some time on the phrase "resignation." But right now, I want to engage you in exploring the concept of winning by never ever giving up. It is not as easy as it sounds.

A woman or a man who will not be denied is a powerful force in this world. So powerful that civilization has developed weapons of mass destruction to combat them. Those weapons are:

■ People will make you feel guilty for your success.

■ People will make you feel guilty or silly for even wanting to be successful.

■ They will talk behind your back.

■ Shun you.

■ Tell you, "You can't."

■ Tell you that has already been tried with disastrous results.

■ Ask you, "Why would you want to do that?"

- Make fun of you.

- Post nasty notes on the Internet about you.

- Talk to the press about you.

- Try to sabotage your efforts.

- Celebrate your defeats.

- Ridicule you.

- Ignore your success.

- Attribute your success to "being lucky."

- Steal credit from you.

- Try to knock you off your course.

- Discourage you.

- Spit on your dreams.

- Lay traps for you.

- Beat you when you are down.

These are truly weapons of mass destruction.

Rudyard Kipling, in his great poem *If*, has a line that says **"If you can meet with triumph and disaster and treat those two imposters just the same."** Rudy (as his friends called him) was right. In a long, and ultimately successful career, you will meet the twin imposters of triumph and disaster. To win, you must never ever give up.

I am always amazed at the difference a few years can make. I am old enough to remember Richard Nixon losing the presidential election and then losing the election for the governorship of California. He did not just lose the governor's race, he was really nasty to the press on his way out the door. **"You won't have Nixon to kick around anymore. . . ."** And yet, he ended up being elected President of the United States of America twice. Go figure.

Designated *for Success*

When I look at my own career, I have been up and I have been down. I have moved ahead at breakneck speed and I have hit plateaus that lasted, in one case, eight long years. I have had bitter disappointments. A few failures. Lots of opportunities to say, "It's just not worth it."

I have noticed several traits shared by those who fully reach their dreams in life. Some of them are talented beyond belief. Some are really fortunate. Most are just plain doggedly tenacious.

I know that people do not just wake up one day and become doggedly tenacious. For some of you, your biggest challenge will be overcoming the tendency to give up when you get discouraged. How do you overcome that tendency? I do not think it is easy to overcome, but let us discuss it a bit.

The first step in toughening your resolve is to decide to do just that—toughen your resolve. It is a conscientious decision that you can make. Once you have made up your mind, you will probably need someone to support you in your efforts. Choose wisely. Few people are tough enough to help you. Find someone who is.

Next, take on some risky ventures outside of work. Not risky enough to cause you permanent harm if you fail. However, they need to be risky enough to put something at stake. Here is the best part—you cannot really fail at these activities, because even in the failing, you will learn to pick yourself up and continue pursuing your goal.

For me, my way of taking personal risks has been marathoning. I am built like a middle linebacker and was a sprinter and hurdler in college. I am definitely **not** built to run 26.2 miles in a few hours' time. Yet, I have completed nearly a dozen marathons so far, including the Pikes Peak Marathon. The Pikes Peak Marathon starts at 6,500 feet altitude, goes up to the summit of Pikes Peak at 14,110 feet, and then returns to the bottom of the mountain. It is a bitch. I finished it at age 46 years. It was not pretty, but I finished.

Marathoning gives me multiple opportunities to quit. Anyone who has ever run one will know exactly what I mean. The chances of working months for something that may end in failure are fairly high. And, since I brag to everyone that I am going to run the marathon, it would be pretty public if I failed. Even though I have finished every one I have started, I have always been willing to fail. Recovering from failure is a very valuable lesson.

Marathoning is not for everyone. There are hundreds of risky ventures out there:

- Write a book.

- Give a speech.

- Take on a project that no one else has been able to complete.

- Run for office.

- Run a charity and set a high goal for fund raising.

- Run an important event.

- Climb a mountain.

- Float a river.

- Learn to fly a plane.

- Land a part in a play.

Whatever you do, learn something from it. Focus on what it takes to be successful. Feel what it is like to be successful. Experience discouragement and deal with it. Experience a failure and come to realize that the world goes on. A word about failure. . . .

Have you ever done any genealogy work? If you have, you know that it is extremely hard to find out anything about anyone that lived prior to your great-grandparents. You can find out when and where they were born and died. You can get their marriage records and find them in census listings. But try to find out what their biggest failure was in life. You cannot! Failure (unless it is spectacular) does not mean very much. The memory of it dies out quickly. Failure is just an opportunity to show the world how tough you are. It gives you an opportunity to prove that you will not be denied.

I have a friend, Lynn Lyen, who points out (accurately I might add) that neither failure nor lack of ability has ever slowed me down. He is right. I consider it my biggest strength.

"Because a fellow has failed once or twice or a dozen times, you don't want to set him down as a failure till he's dead or loses his courage."

—George Horace Lorimer

■ Chapter 12

If

by Rudyard Kipling

If you can keep your head when all about you

Are losing theirs and blaming it on you;

If you can trust yourself when all men doubt you,

But make allowance for their doubting too;

If you can wait and not be tired by waiting,

Or, being lied about, don't deal in lies;

Or, being hated, don't give way to hating,

And yet don't look too good, nor talk too wise;

If you can dream—and not make dreams your master;

If you can think—and not make thoughts your aim;

If you can meet with triumph and disaster

And treat those two imposters just the same;

If you can bear to hear the truth you've spoken

Twisted by knaves to make a trap for fools,

Or watch the things you gave your life to broken,

And stoop to build 'em up with wornout tools;

If you can make one heap of all your winnings

And risk it on one turn of pitch-and-toss;

And lose, and start again at your beginnings

And never breathe a word about your loss;

If you can force your heart and nerve and sinew

To serve your turn long after they are gone,

And so hold on when there is nothing in you

Except the Will which says to them, "Hold on";

If you can talk with crowds and keep your virtue,

Or walk with kings—nor lose the common touch;

If neither foes nor loving friends can hurt you;

If all men count with you, but none too much;

If you can fill the unforgiving minute

With sixty seconds' worth of distance run—

Yours is the Earth and everything that's in it,

And—which is more—you'll be a Man my son!

Designated *for Success*

Part Two—
How to Lose

*"You are beaten to earth? Well, well,
what's that? Come up with a smiling
face. It's nothing against you to fall
down flat, but to lie there—that's
disgrace."*

—Edmund Vance Cooke

Designated *for Success*

■ Chapter 13
How to Lose

■ ■ ■ ■ ■ ■ ■ ■ ■ ■ ■ ■ ■ ■ ■ ■ ■ ■

"Forget past mistakes. Forget failures. Forget everything except what you're to do now and do it. Today is your lucky day."

—Will Durant

■ ■ ■ ■ ■ ■ ■ ■ ■ ■ ■ ■ ■ ■ ■ ■ ■ ■

There are traps out there…traps set to throw you off your course. You have probably already stepped into several of these traps by now. We all have. If you begin to recognize them, you can do something to avoid them the next time around.

Run into Trouble . . . Blame Others

■ ■ ■ ■ ■ ■ ■ ■ ■ ■ ■ ■ ■ ■ ■ ■ ■ ■

"Admitting error clears the score, and proves you wiser than before."

—Arthur Guiterman

■ ■ ■ ■ ■ ■ ■ ■ ■ ■ ■ ■ ■ ■ ■ ■ ■ ■

I am always amazed at most people's inability to simply say "I screwed up." Why is that so difficult to say? We all screw up eventually. If you did screw up, all the rest of us know it already. And some of us can hardly wait for you to blame it on someone else. When you fall into that nasty trap, you not only get credit for the screw up, people lose trust in you at the same time. Kind of a package debacle.

When I am interviewing people for a job, I always ask them to discuss two or three of their biggest mistakes. After I assure them that I am not interested in hearing more about their "big mistake" of caring too much, working too hard, or being too loyal, I repeat the question in more basic terms. "What have you really screwed up?" I ask. The most common answer is, "I can't really think of anything right now." Bull!

I like risk takers. If you are a risk taker, you have made a mistake or two. Tell me about those mistakes. My next, and more important, question will be, "What did you do to recover from that mistake?" Now we are getting into some interesting territory.

If you are going to work for 40 or 50 years and reach for the very top of your profession, you will make a mistake or two or 10 . . . count on it. Accept responsibility. Recover and get on with your life.

Suspect yourself. Do not blame the world, the economy, your co-workers, your boss, the lack of support you get at home, your difficult childhood, the new allergy medicine you are taking, or bad data from the Marketing Department. Accept responsibility even if you know you are not 100 percent to blame.

■ ■ ■ ■ ■ ■ ■ ■ ■ ■ ■ ■ ■ ■ ■ ■ ■ ■ ■

"A man may fall many times, but he won't be a failure until he says that someone pushed him."

—Elmer G. Letterman

■ ■ ■ ■ ■ ■ ■ ■ ■ ■ ■ ■ ■ ■ ■ ■ ■ ■ ■

■ Chapter 14
Do Not Accept Help

"No one can whistle a symphony. It takes an orchestra to play it."

—H. E. Luccock

There are a lot of uncoachable people in the world . . . people who do not want your help and will never ask for it. Let us, for the moment, call these folks "losers."

We live in a complex world. Most things worth doing take teams of people to get the project done. Most of your own work can be speeded along or improved with the assistance of others. So why is it that some people absolutely refuse to ask for or accept the help of others?

I had the wonderful opportunity to attend a several-week-long graduate course at Harvard University. We lived on campus. We worked together in small teams. It was the educational experience of my lifetime.

I learned a lot from the course content. More importantly, I learned how valuable it was to learn together, as part of a team. We met in the evening to do our assignments together. We split up the work and counted on each other to do a great job on our part of the assignment. We held each other accountable for doing that work. We met before class to do our final preparations. Together, we presented our solutions. I have never learned so much so quickly.

We live in a diverse world. Limiting ourselves to our own narrow views or set of experiences is a waste of potential. We are better together than we are on our own.

Have you ever taken a course on diversity? The best ones I have taken focus on the business reason for embracing diversity. I watched one company I worked for explode with growth and profitability once it learned that the rest of the world was not all white and all male.

My old company began to embrace America as America is configured, with people from every part of the globe. It hired salespeople who spoke several languages. It advertised in Spanish and Korean media. It started up inner-city strategic partnerships. And sales went through the roof.

We often think we have all the answers. Our egos get in the way of accepting help. Our own stubborn nature stands in the way. Put these all aside. Get all the help you can. Winners accept help. They accept coaching. They work as part of a team. They are open to the ideas of others.

"No one can be the best at everything. But when all of us combine our talents, we can be the best at virtually anything."

—Don Ward

■ Chapter 15
Become Resigned

"*Misery is a communicable disease.*"

—Martha Graham

I am not writing about the kind of resignation that leaves you with no job. I am writing about resignation that leaves you with no hope. Resignation is a deep-rooted disease that takes millions of people off of the success track and then out of the game.

Resignation is not just giving up. People who give up get up to try again later. People who are resigned can be permanently resigned. They believe they are powerless. They believe they are injured. They have given up deep down to their bone marrow.

Why is resignation so toxic? Because it is communicable. You can catch it. In fact, you can help get it going in the first place. People who are resigned individuals need volunteers to help them wallow around in their despair. You could be that person.

Several years ago I moved into an office filled with resigned people. I would talk to them about being the best. They would look at me as if I had just landed from outer space. I would talk to them about winning. They would tell me how unfair they had been treated. I would say "Let us try something new." They would say, "We have already done that and it did not work." It was the single-most frustrating time of my life.

Somewhere along the way I met a woman named Loretta Malandro. She helped me understand the nature of resignation. And since Loretta and her associates make their living by helping individuals and teams deal with such important issues as resignation, I will not attempt to steal their work with my few words on the subject. In the back of the book you will find out how to get in touch with Loretta Malandro and her organization. But, let me give you "resignation lite."

We are all subject to becoming resigned. The important part is to recognize when resignation is present for you or for those around you. If you can master that task, you can move on to recovery and put resignation behind you.

To be resigned, you need to become a victim. A victim feels that there is nothing he or she can do (or the price to do it is too high) to change the situation. To become a victim you will also need to find someone who is persecuting you. A likely candidate is your boss, management, or "the company." It is also helpful to have a co-conspirator or enabler to sympathize with you and reinforce your feelings of helplessness.

Victims love to be right. They love to blame others. They do nothing to solve problems. They are actually invested in keeping those problems alive . . . so they can continue to be right and to blame.

I mentioned that the disease is communicable. It is highly contagious. The victim can have an enormous impact on others. The more victims who join the party, the more they can reinforce one another's feelings of helplessness. They can collect evidence together to "prove" their point.

Things victims say:

- ■ "No one ever listens to me."

- ■ "He will never change."

- ■ "I guess I am not important."

- ■ "Here we go again. Another program of the day."

- ■ "We did that years ago. It didn't work then, it won't work now."

- ■ "Just ignore her. We can outlive her. She is just like all the bosses before her."

Designated *for Success*

- "I do not believe the numbers. They are hiding the real facts."

- "That is impossible."

So, suspect yourself. Ask yourself if you have become resigned about anything. Such as:

- "They will never let a woman become a senior executive around here."

- "I could not possibly get a college degree at this late date."

- "The only ones who ever get promoted to senior management are the friends of the owner."

- "I am black. Do you see any black senior executives around here? Fat chance."

- "No one will ever let me run a profit center because I am from Sales."

- "We could never match the competition's price."

- "They are too far ahead of us. Let us quit worrying about becoming number one and focus on holding on to second place."

- "I am not even going to ask for a raise. I know that cheapskate will never give me one."

Any of those sound familiar? If so, you have visited or been around resignation. So, what can you do about it?

First of all, you can develop your own radar that looks for resignation in yourself and in those around you. You can also ask your coach or teammates to help you detect your areas of resignation. Just reading these few words will probably make you more aware of resignation for the rest of your life.

Once you detect resignation, it becomes a matter of recovery. It is a mindset that says you will not allow yourself to sit on the sidelines. You will not enable others to do so. You will, instead, look for the possibility. Remember Robert Kennedy (who was quoting George Bernard Shaw), ***"Some look at things that are, and ask why. I dream of things that never were and ask why not?"*** That is the difference between resignation and possibility.

I know it is tempting to join in the wallowing sometimes. We have all done it. It makes you seem like one of the gang. It gives you a common foe. Next time that opportunity presents itself, think about what you are doing. You are becoming a co-conspirator for resignation. Winners are not resigned.

Think about it with some plain old good sense. Which is valued more by a company, a victim who sees no way to improve the present situation, or someone who can see possibility in the situation and who has the guts to try something different to achieve a better outcome? The good pay and good jobs go to people who think about possibilities, not to victims.

Perfection is pretty hard to come by in this world. Things do get screwed up. Some things stayed screwed up a long time. But, achieving perfection on the first pass is not the real goal. It is to get to perfection as soon as possible. So when things get out of whack, watch out for the resignation—in you and in those around you. When you find it, recover and begin to look for the possibilities for getting it right the next time around. And one last little bit of advice. If you have chronic victims in your organization . . . get rid of them. They are contagious.

I forgot the biggest resignation of them all—the "I am too old" resignation. I am hearing that one more and more these days. Could it have anything to do with the fact that my generation is now in our mid-50s?

"I am too old" is complete hogwash. The gentleman who runs one of the most successful insurance companies in the world, Hank Greenberg of AIG, is in his 70s. He did not start to have his major success until he was in his 50s.

I know companies that run you out the door in your 50s. So what. There are lots of companies hiring experienced professionals at that age. If you think you are too old, you are. If you think you have still got it, you do. "I am too old" is just plain not true. Forget about it!

"*Resignation is a kind of suspended animation.*"

—Frank Patalano

Designated *for Success*

■ Chapter 16
Work in a Vacuum

■ ■ ■ ■ ■ ■ ■ ■ ■ ■ ■ ■ ■ ■ ■ ■ ■

"It is well to remember that the entire universe, with one trifling exception, is composed of others."

—Andrew Holmes

■ ■ ■ ■ ■ ■ ■ ■ ■ ■ ■ ■ ■ ■ ■ ■ ■

A nother surefire way to lose is to become isolated. Watch out for this one. It sneaks up on you. It fools you. It can finally crush you.

I worked for one company for 27 years. It was, and is, a fine company. It was huge, with tens of thousands of employees. This fine company had and has the ability to completely isolate an individual, and it does. How is this possible?

Over the years, large and not-so-large organizations build up a culture. The culture at the company I used to work for was "Everything you need to know is right here." In large part, it was right. It had and has great resources.

About five years into my career, I realized that I was meeting virtually no one outside of my company. Some of my neighbors and friends seemed to be progressing faster in their careers than I was. They seemed to be earning more money. They seemed to be doing a wider range of activities.

I started going to industry luncheons. Wow . . . what an eye opener! There was a whole new world out there. Pretty soon I ran out of opportunities to tag along to these luncheons as a guest. It was time to actually become involved in these outside activities.

My old company would deny it strongly, but it not too subtly discouraged outside involvement by their employees, except in charitable work. But, since it did not say "no" outright, I took a chance. I joined an industry luncheon group. I also signed up for a series of courses and examinations that might one day lead to my earning a CPCU designation. I knew that designation would give me entrée to monthly meetings and a variety of other outside activities.

You could almost hear the "pop" as I broke out of my vacuum. I had a regional vice president of my firm sit me down and tell me to, "Knock off all this outside educational crap." In fact, when I decided to add the CLU designation to my list of accomplishments, he refused to have the company pay for it, even though it was a company benefit. His reasoning was that I was preparing myself to leave the company. And he was right. I stormed out of there—**20 years later.**

I see a very dangerous habit creep into some peoples lives. I call it the "in-bin syndrome." Most people just work their in-bins. They do not look up and around to understand and appreciate what is really going on. They look to the left side of their desk or take a look into their e-mails, note any new work to be done, and do that work. That is what they do day after day and year after year.

If you work your in-bins exclusively, you are working someone else's agenda. The ironic thing is that the people setting your agenda do not even have an agenda in mind for you, other than "Do this work." It is reacting and never proacting.

Have you become vacuum sealed? What do you know about the department next door? What do you know about the competitor down the street? Is what you know restricted to what you pick up in industry periodicals, newspapers, television, and the Internet? What about learning something from actual people—people with whom you could build a relationship?

I am convinced that you cannot achieve your highest dreams alone. It may be alright to spend the majority of your time working your in-bin and concentrating on the environment in which you work. But, do not fall into the trap of letting that become **all** you do.

My first surprise, when I started to navigate outside my company, was that not all the people I met from my competitors were evil doers. I had been led to believe that these people were unethical, uncaring, classless dolts who really should be avoided at all costs. It turns out they were just about the same as the people at my company. I also learned that they had some real misconceptions about the people with whom I worked. We opened up communications.

Jim Strohl was the first boss I had who had not been raised in our company. Jim had actually worked for several insurance companies before joining our then-current company. He actually had outside contacts. He put me in touch with those people—an eye-opening experience.

I worked for years in an office with tile floors, grey desks, and no pictures on the walls. Jim sent me to the regional office of one of his old companies to get some information he felt we needed. When I arrived at the office, I immediately noticed several things. The floors were carpeted. Everyone had a work cubicle. There were oil paintings on the walls. They had a workout facility and a bowling alley. They had an indoor pool. Life was much different at this new place.

Jim introduced me to a fellow who held basically the same job that I had at my company. During the course of our conversation, he asked me what I paid my underwriters. I told him. He looked surprised. He asked how much I paid my supervisors. Same reaction. He wanted to know what I paid my managers. When I told him he became visibly upset. There was a long silence. Then he said "I hate to ask, but what do you make?" I told him. More silence. Finally, he said, "I just figured out who is paying for the artwork around here." It turns out that I was making 25 percent more that he was.

I'm not sure why Jim sent me to see this man. I suspect that he knew how much better we were paid than others in the industry, and wanted me to learn that first-hand. It worked. I began to see things differently. I began to realize that all jobs have certain trade-offs. The grass is not always greener "over there."

Jim is a different kind of guy. On his first day on the job, he recommended that all employees read *North Dallas Forty*. He did that because everyone was complaining about our work conditions at the time. When you read *North Dallas Forty*, a fictional but realistic book about life in professional football, you just cannot help but feel better about your own working conditions.

If you want to be the best at something, do not assume that "the best" resides at your current company. That could be the case, but I doubt it. Go out and see the world. See what the best really looks like. Break out of your self-inflicted solitary confinement. There is a big world out there and you need to experience as much of it as you can.

"When you look at the world in a narrow way, how narrow it seems! When you look at it in a mean way, how mean it seems! When you look at it selfishly, how selfish it is! But when you look at it in a broad, generous, friendly spirit, what wonderful people you find in it."

—Horace Rutledge

■ Chapter 17
Think Short Term

"*The great thing in this world is not so much where you stand, as in what direction you are moving.*"

—Oliver Wendell Holmes

ecoming the best at something . . . the absolute top of your profession . . . that does not happen overnight. Athletes can become the absolute best in just a few years. But, most other professions take decades to reach the top. In fact, once you get to the top, I have been told that you find there is still much more to learn. Reaching your life's dream may take a lifetime. Who cares what minor unfairness came across your path today?

Have you ever heard the saying **"Whoever said life was fair?"** I have a bit of a twist on that saying. I look for nothing to be fair in the short run. I believe that virtually everything will turn out to be fair in the long run. That little philosophy has seen me through some bleak days. I play for the long run.

Let us take a look at some short-term land mines:

- The nincompoop next to you gets promoted.

- One of the members of your team—the one that did no work—grabs all the credit for the successful project.

- You get screwed on your raise.

- ■ You are paid less than the person who just joined the company with less experience than you.

- ■ You get screwed on your bonus.

- ■ Everyone gets acknowledged for good work except you.

- ■ Your buddies are invited to the boss's house for dinner and you are not.

- ■ The CEO comes to town and you do not get to meet her.

- ■ You are passed over for a big project team.

- ■ You are passed over for making officer in your company.

- ■ You are not invited to the educational seminar in Florida.

These kinds of things happen all of the time. I do not like them any better than you do. They irritate the hell out of me. However, I have learned to laugh at these short-term events and get on with my life.

I do not care one whit about winning anything in the short run. However, I want to win everything in the long run.

I mention confidence throughout this book. I do so because I think it is a key factor for success. Being able to put up with the unfair events that will tumble your way on a regular basis throughout your career has a lot to do with being confident. If you know you are a better person for the job than the yahoo they chose, have the confidence to let the world turn a few times. Yahoos get found out. *Real talent always gets discovered. Play for the long run.*

I have watched hundreds of equally talented, lesser talented, and no-talent people pass me by in my career. I have caught up to and passed every one. The ones that have stayed ahead of me probably deserve to stay ahead of me. (I do not actually believe that statement. I just wrote it to sound nice.) However, life is long and I suspect I will learn enough to someday pass even them.

The hardest short-term slights to put up with are the ones that involve morally corrupt people. I mean the cheaters, the stealers, and the abusers. These people absolutely gain advantage from their dastardly deeds . . . in the short run. But just as absolutely, they get found out. And when the day of reckoning arrives, watch how far and how fast they fall. Take no pleasure in their fall (just kidding). And

Designated *for Success*

use the lesson to reinforce your commitment to playing for the long run. You **will** win in the end.

"Time is a great manager: it arranges things well."

—Pierre Corneille

■ Chapter 18
Let a Bad Boss Run You Out of Town

"We conquer by continuing."

—George Matheson

You are probably going to lose your wallet, a credit card, or your driver's license several times in your life. Poop happens. Deal with it.

It is the same with bosses. You are probably going to run into several horrible bosses during a lifetime of work. If you are self-employed, you will run into several people who stand in the way of your success—a critic, a buyer that tries to make your life a living hell, or an agent that treats you like a loser. The trick is to plan for this eventuality and have a game plan for living through it.

If you are new to the world of business, you may have no perspective on what constitutes a bad boss. Let me give you some hints. A bad boss:

- Treats you like a child, doling out information in teaspoon quantities.

- Sets things up so you are bound to fail, then makes sure to catch you failing.

- Tries to intimidate you.

- Takes credit for your good work.

- Never gives you feedback on your progress.

- Keeps you unaware of your salary range and where you stand in that range.

- Spits on your dreams. In fact, has no idea that you have dreams.

- Narrowly defines your job so you have no room to exercise your talent and to grow.

- Provides you with no training.

- Displays anger and/or threatens you. Makes it uncomfortable for you to come to work.

- Does not listen.

- Is unaware of his or her impact on you or on others.

- Belittles you. Makes you feel unimportant.

- Asks/demands you do things that are unethical or illegal.

- Harasses you.

- Lets others harass you.

If any of the above applies to you, you probably have or had a bad boss. It is not the way it is supposed to be. Most of us have many more great bosses than we do bad bosses. But almost everyone has a bad boss at some point in his or her career.

What to do? The easiest thing to do is to shrink your own game and just try to exist in the job. Remember the section on resignation? Reread it. Resignation is alive and well when a bad boss is present.

The second-most-common reaction is to quit. Imagine that. People quit because they have a bad boss. Who wins in that situation? The bad boss. Never let the bastard win.

My first bad boss was a nice enough person. I like the person to this day. However, he believed in never rocking the ship. He did not rock the ship. He would not let you rock the ship. Everything just kind of stood still in time. He did not get promoted and no one beneath him got promoted. He was a bad boss especially for a young and ambitious person reporting to him.

I made some classic mistakes with the above bad boss. Because I liked him, I never confronted him. I took what came my way, which, of course, was wave after wave of more of the same. I did not grow for years.

I did not maneuver. I just sat there and accepted the status quo. What could I have done? I could have talked to him about the situation. I could have explained the impact he was having on me. I could have asked for his help to get me a more growth-oriented assignment. I could have posted for a job in another department. I could have talked to Human Resources about him (probably a really bad idea). I could have talked to his boss about the situation (yet another poor idea). Instead, I did nothing.

I own something called a ***do nothing*** machine. It was given to me by my friend and co-worker, Dick Hennig. It is a block of wood with two channels carved in it. It has a crank that you can turn that powers another piece of wood to run back and forth in the two channels. Net result: it accomplishes nothing. It came my way after I admitted to myself and did so publicly, that I often fall into periods of ***"do nothing."***

A lot of people do nothing. They take whatever comes their way and accept it for what it is. They see possibilities, but do nothing to cause change to happen. They often get nothing because they do nothing. ***Are you a do nothing?***

To help you answer that question let me ask you some additional questions.

- Are you happy with the amount of training you are getting?

- Are you happy with the challenging assignments coming your way?

- Are you pleased with your progress?

- Do you know how much money you can make in your current job and in the next two jobs above you?

- Do you know what the average salary is in your industry for a similar job?

- Have you gotten a comprehensive performance appraisal in the last 12 months?

- Are you as productive as you know you can be?

- Are you secretly mad at your boss for something that occurred recently or even long ago?

- Is a teammate hurting the overall productivity of your team?

- Are you angry about something at work, but afraid to speak up?

- Have you been treated as fairly as that new person that was just hired (I heard she got a $50,000 signing bonus)?

If any of the above rings true to you, what have you done about it? By the way, complaining to a co-worker or to your spouse does not constitute action. It constitutes resignation.

Do nothings get exactly what they deserve. If you are a periodic or full-time do nothing, do something about it. As CEO of your own career, you are required to act.

A second bad boss I had was just plain incompetent. He was politically protected, but did not know his job. I was afraid I would be painted with the same brush. I considered leaving the company. However, by now I had grown up a bit and decided to excel at my job. I figured that he would finally be found out or that his political cover would fade away. I wanted to be ready when opportunity presented itself. And that is just how it worked out.

My boss's boss saw me as a loyal employee who cared enough to do a great job even though I had no role model. In fact, he stepped in and became my role model and a coach. When I had grown enough, he found another spot for my boss and moved me into his job. I had planted no knives in my old boss's back. We remain friends to this day. I got ahead because I did the work to earn the promotion.

A third bad boss was an intimidator. The first day you worked for him, he would set you straight as to who was the boss. I think you take on intimidators the first and every time they try to intimidate you. Most are bullies. Most bullies fold like a house of cards once you show them that you will not take their crap. Mine folded. I got along very well with him after that first tense encounter.

Be a little careful here. There is a fine line between an intimidator (bad boss) and a taskmaster (potentially great boss). Taskmasters just will not accept anything less than your best performance. They will be straight with you and tell you when you have disappointed them or the team. They will hold you accountable and run you out of town if you cannot perform up to standards. There is nothing wrong with taskmasters. I respect them.

Intimidators are out to make you fail on even the most trivial assignments. They want you to be aware of the horrible consequences of crossing some hard-to-define line of conduct. They are out to scare you **whether you are performing well or not.** They love to tear your work down to your face or to others. They love to wad up your expense account and send it back to you in a ball with a yellow sticky attached that says "Get real!" They cannot wait to send a real or imagined report on your alleged malfeasance to your personnel file. They love to say "Don, as soon as this meeting is over, I want you to come to my office to explain why you deliberately chose to ignore my request for full information on the progress of your project." My favorite intimidation tactic is letting it be known that they are interviewing people for your job.

Stand up to these creeps. Ninety-nine percent of them will be found out and get their just desserts in the end. The other 1 percent will probably end up running a small country somewhere. Life is not fair.

Do not let a bad boss run you off. Have confidence. Do something positive about your situation. Do not listen to the siren song of resignation. Do not become a do nothing. Do outlive the bastard.

"*Let us then be up and doing,*
With a heart for any fate;
Still achieving, still pursuing,
Long to labor and to wait."

—Henry Wadsworth Longfellow

■ Chapter 19
Become Comfortable

"Too many people are thinking of security instead of opportunity. They seem more afraid of life than death."

—James F. Byrnes

Settling kills the dream. Settle for something comfortable and you have just given up. You may be happy today, but you will also know that you could have done so much better. The word "regret" will visit you on a regular basis. Winners don't let themselves become comfortable short of their full goal.

I had a group of branch managers who worked for me. These were and are terrific people. They control a profit center. They hire and fire. They motivate and train. They make some serious money. About 350 days of the year, they are the boss. Those few other days they are usually in a small group of their fellow branch managers listening to the likes of me. Being a branch manager is a very tough and a very good job.

I talked to the branch managers about their careers. I asked them a few questions: "How many of you set out in life to be a branch manager? Is becoming a branch manager your childhood dream? Is this what you really want to accomplish in your life?"

I asked them these questions because I suspected several of them had become comfortable. If I am right, some of them have climbed a long way up the corporate ladder and found a comfortable spot to rest. They took a look up to the top and decided that it was just too hard to make the final push. So they rested. They gave up short of their goal. Stopped dreaming.

You should have heard their replies! Silence. Not a word. Why? Because they may have never had to confront the truth before. Because my question gave them pause for thought. Because it probably made a few of them pretty angry—at me or at themselves.

I am angry too. I get angry when I see people waste their potential by becoming comfortable. My theory is: First you are comfortable. Then you are resigned.

You start saying to yourself:

- "I guess my time has passed."

- "It is just too risky to give up what I have got for something unknown. I know I can do this job."

- "Management is blind. If they knew what they were doing, I would be president by now."

- "I'm getting too old for this. No one would take a chance on me now."

- "Those lucky kids with the master's degrees get all the good jobs."

- "Don's going to pick one of his friends over me every single time."

- "I never have a nervous day anymore. I have this job down pat."

- "The company will never promote me. I am too valuable here."

Tennessee Williams said *"Security is a kind of death."* I agree. It is a bit like my least favorite play in football, the prevent defense. Every time I see a football team decide to let the opposing team get good long gains, while guarding against a touchdown play, I just shake my head. If it is a team I care about, I start yelling at the television. (This is not too bright, but it makes me feel better.) Guess what— those good long gains usually turn into touchdowns anyway.

There is no security in standing still. It may feel secure. But I have been around long enough to see well-qualified branch managers with long records of growth and profit replaced to "shake things up" or "to give someone else a chance." You may think that kind of change is stupid. But it does happen and it happens a lot. The only security comes from rising up so high in an organization or profession that you get to call the shots. Those kinds of positions are scarce. However, if you are on top or moving up the professional ladder, you have more security than those beneath you. Comfortable may seem safe. But it is not.

And there is another type of comfort that is also dangerous. I call it the "sofa."

My uncle Pat McDonald is a man that I admire. He was the leader of his class at Annapolis. Pat had a distinguished naval career in the nuclear Navy. He retired early and eventually became CEO of a company that ran nuclear energy facilities in the South. I listen carefully to his advice.

Several years ago Pat invited me to Alabama to visit that state's electrical power production facilities. It gave us time to share ideas and for me to learn something about his business. As we were driving to a fossil fuel facility, he asked me how long I had been with my company. I told him that I had been there 25 years. He replied that I was a "sofa."

"A what?"

"A sofa."

He went on to explain that I was like a valued piece of furniture—useful, fit in nicely, comfortable, and taken for granted. To tell the truth, I was insulted. To dig down to the real truth, he was right.

Organizations and professions are like pyramids. Lots of people start out to become the top person. Some make it a long way up the pyramid. At some point, most quit climbing, fall, or are pushed off. A few make it to the top. A few are left on a high plateau, wanting to go higher but finding themselves blocked. At that point, if you are useful, fit in nicely, and are comfortable, you become a sofa.

How is your comfort level? Have you settled? Did you set out to be the chairman and ended up the branch manager? **Have you become a sofa?**

If you find you did listen to the siren song of comfort or your way is blocked, do something about it. **Time to bust a move.** Talk to your boss. Tell him or her that you are open for change. Take a risk. Move to a new company or a new department. Do not just sit there and expect a miracle. It is time to start climbing to the top.

"The only peace, the only security, is in fulfillment."

—Henry Miller

■ Chapter 20
"I Am Too Busy"

"In putting off what one has to do, one runs the risk of never being able to do it."

—Charles Baudelaire

I tend to ask people a lot of questions, especially people I care about the most. Such as:

- ■ "Why not go back to school and get that degree?"

- ■ "Why not join a volunteer organization and get some practice managing and leading?"

- ■ "Why not get your professional designation?"

- ■ "Why not volunteer to take on the big assignment?"

- ■ "Why aren't you a speaker at the upcoming event?"

The answer I most often get is: "I am too busy."

In fact, I usually get the long form of "I am too busy," which includes details on the golf league they are in, the need to coach their kids' hockey team, the fact that they have two young children, or they are training for a marathon. I am quite sure that not one of these people ever considered the fact that he or she had just insulted me.

I say "insulted me" because I have had young kids. I have been involved in the kids' activities. I went back to school and got more education. I have run marathons. I am a very busy boy. So what makes them busier than me? They are not busier. They are making a choice. I respect that choice if they call it what it is—a choice.

Consider this.

You will never have more time on your hands than you have today. I can remember training for a marathon the week my daughter was born. I also took several exams for my CPCU designation that week. I was fully employed and managing something like 100 people. I thought I was busy.

Today my kids are grown and on their own. I am still training for a marathon. I am taking no classes. However, I am an executive with a major insurance company and I am busier in my mid-50s than at any other point in my life.

If you are too busy now, you will be too busy all the rest of your life. "I am too busy" is a poor excuse.

And get used to being busy. If you are going to be great, you are going to be busy. The trick is to prioritize and to work your butt off, as needed.

The next time you hear yourself saying that you are too busy, suspect yourself. Suspect that you are making an excuse. Suspect that you are trying to stay comfortable. Suspect that you are not pushing yourself toward that lifelong dream. As the person in charge of your career, you owe it to yourself to not let "I am too busy" get in the way of your success.

■ ■ ■ ■ ■ ■ ■ ■ ■ ■ ■ ■ ■ ■ ■ ■ ■

"Sweat plus sacrifice equals success."

—Charles O. Finley

■ ■ ■ ■ ■ ■ ■ ■ ■ ■ ■ ■ ■ ■ ■ ■ ■

■ Chapter 21
Confuse Setback with Failure

"The fellow who never makes a mistake takes his orders from one who does."

—Herbert B. Prochnow

At age 22, I was the youngest underwriter in our office. I really wanted to contribute to the group effort. I wanted to earn every penny of the fabulous $125 a week I was being paid. I tried to make up for my lack of knowledge and experience with my enthusiasm and hard work.

Word came that the home office was coming to town. There was going to be an audit. I asked around. What kinds of things would it be looking for? I was told that it would check to make sure the work found in our files met the standards set forth in our underwriting guides.

Problem. Our underwriting guides were a mess. The updates had never been filed. They looked sloppy. They were not even labeled. Ah hah! An opportunity to be of service.

I came into the office on Saturday to fix our library of manuals. I worked all day long, alone and happy in my work. I filed all the updates, straightened up the books on the shelves, and made everything look first-class. It took me eight unpaid hours.

The last thing I did was get out the labeling machine and label every one of the manuals. I used big letters so you could see them across the room. I labeled the Underwriting Manuel, the Workers Compensation Manuel, the Auto Manuel, and on and on.

On Monday I arrived a few minutes late. The entire office was gathered around my handy work and laughing hysterically. Turns out that "manual" is not spelled m-a-n-u-e-l.

Who knew?

I had just made a fool out of myself to all the people that meant the most to me in my young career. In fact, they gave me the nick name "Manuel" right then and there. I was known as Manuel for years. Some of those folks still call me Manuel.

That was the first of my mistakes. There would be many more. There will be many more. I tend to move quickly and there is some breaking of glass involved. It is important to put mistakes into perspective.

For example, I get feedback about being a pretty good public speaker. I have thought about why. And I think it is because I have learned to forgive myself. If I get up without notes and speak for an hour, it is likely that I may forget to say something I had planned to say. Rather than worry about it, I forgive myself. I try to learn something from it. Perhaps it will cause me to use notes next time around.

When I am getting ready to go on stage, I am fairly calm. I know that whatever happens, life will go on. I will probably do a very good job and I may even do a terrific job. Either way, I will also probably mess up a joke or leave out an important part. It will be okay.

What about a big mistake? I am reminded of the oft-quoted thought from President Theodore Roosevelt. He said:

> The credit belongs to the man who is actually in the arena, whose face is marred by dust and sweat and blood, who strives valiantly; who errs and comes short again and again . . . ; who knows the great enthusiasm, the great devotion, who spends himself in a worthy cause, who at the best knows in the end the triumph of high achievement and who at the worst if he fails, at least he fails while daring greatly. So that his place shall never be with those cold and timid souls who know neither victory nor defeat.

Designated *for Success*

Take a careful look at the leaders of your organization or of your profession. Do you know them well? If you do, you probably know the mistakes they have made on their way to the top. In fact, you may be amazed at how they ever overcame some of those mistakes.

Poop happens. You will make a mistake or two. Some of them may be big and may have significant consequences. Take your medicine and get back on track. A setback is not a failure.

"Our mistakes will not irreparably damage our lives unless we let them."

—James E. Sweaney

Designated *for Success*

Part Three—How to Recover
(The Art and Science of Losing a Job or Facing a Setback)

"For a long time, it had seemed to me that life was about to begin—real life. But there was always some obstacle in the way. Something to be got through first, some unfinished business, time still to be served, a debt to be paid. Then life would begin. At last, it dawned on me that these obstacles were my life."

—Friar Alfred D'Souza

Designated *for Success*

■ Chapter 22
All Rumors Are True

"I believe that all rumors are true. It is the details that turn out to be wrong. And the details are important."

—Donald J. Hurzeler, CPCU, CLU

Okay. It may not be kosher to quote one's self, but I could not find a good quote about rumors. And I have been saying the above sentences for years. We should all listen to rumors.

Have you been hearing rumors at your company? That is how it starts.

- ■ "I hear we are up for sale."

- ■ "The big boys have been meeting with lawyers and investors behind closed doors for several days."

- ■ "I saw the CEO of our biggest competitor sneaking into our CEO's office at about 6 p.m. last night."

- ■ "They are working on an early retirement package as we speak. I heard it from my buddy in Human Resources."

- ■ "The paper says that they are going to eliminate 1,500 jobs here."

- ■ "Looks like that multi-national company is going to buy us."

- "Where are all the officers? I hear they are meeting with the company that's buying us."

- "Did that guy say he is with Goldman Sachs?"

- "I heard they are going to fire everyone making over $100,000 a year and all the secretaries."

- "I hear the package they are going to offer gives us three years of full pay and medical benefits for life."

- "I hear there is no package. I know for a fact that they just took delivery of 2,000 moving boxes. They are throwing us out on the street."

Those are the rumors I think you should listen to. Why? Because none of them are entirely true. Live long enough and you will hear each of these rumors several times. But buried in those rumors are grains of truth. You can benefit from those grains of truth. I listen to rumors. I try not to repeat them. I do not take them as completely accurate.

The main benefit of hearing a rumor is to give you time to think through your position so you can start to protect yourself. Protect yourself—an often overlooked concept.

If something is changing at your company, there will almost always be rumors first. If the same rumor persists, it will probably get closer and closer to the truth. If rumors get strong enough, they paralyze the workplace. Do not let this paralysis visit you.

In the face of strong rumors, do two things. First, be seen as doing your best work. There is opportunity in chaos (more later). Second, protect yourself.

Let us explore the idea of protecting yourself.

Protecting yourself is about being prepared for whatever comes your way. The rumors may be entirely wrong. They probably are entirely wrong. But that is no reason not to protect yourself.

I worked in an environment that was filled with rumors. Each rumor was nastier than the last. And, as kind of an insider, I knew that each of the rumors was partially true. So I called together my whole team and said "protect yourself." I told them that there was change in the air. I told them that the change was out of their and my control. I let them know that there was a possibility that some of them could lose their jobs.

I spent time with them explaining what they could do to protect themselves. They could:

1. Network inside and outside the company. Make sure their network is up and operating.

2. Be aware of new job opportunities inside and outside the company.

3. Update their résumés.

4. Practice interviewing. (I offered to interview them for practice.)

5. Think through their situation. What would they do if they lost their job?

6. Think twice before making any long-term commitments, like buying a new house.

7. Take a look at their finances to make sure they had their debt under control and some cash in reserve.

8. Do their best at work.

I shared my observations about how the process of losing a job works. Some members of my team had been with the company for 35 years. They had never lost a job.

I took a lot of criticism for preparing my people. Not from the people. The people did not thank me. But they understood that I was there to be of help in good times or bad. People outside our area thought that you should not stir things up with such talk. You should wait and stir things up with a surprise termination notice. I respectfully disagree.

"*The ultimate measure of a man is not where he stands in moments of comfort and convenience, but where he stands at times of challenge and controversy.*"

—Dr. Martin Luther King, Jr.

■ Chapter 23
The Divorce You Did Not Ask For . . . Getting Fired

"When one door closes, another opens. But we often look so regretfully upon the closed door that we don't see the one that has opened for us."

—Helen Keller

I got fired once. Not really fired, but abandoned. My company sold the part of the company that I had worked in for 27 years to another company. It felt awful.

I was writing a newspaper column at the time and decided to take some notes, to perhaps use later on in a column or two. I took good notes. I observed to the best of my ability the process of losing a job. I never wrote the columns, but I did find my notes. Here is what I observed.

Losing one's job is a process. There are stages to the process. After speaking on this topic for about a decade and getting feedback from those audiences, I am convinced that the process I will describe is pretty much universal.

Stages of Losing a Job

1. Concern

2. Fear

3. Preliminary Acceptance

4. Mourning

5. Waiting

6. Hope

7. Hope Dashed

8. Fear Realized

9. Deer in the Headlights

10. Denial

11. Anger

12. Acceptance

13. Panic

14. Game Plan

15. Work the Game Plan

16. Success

Concern
Concern is the first breath of change. People start acting out of pattern. Long-planned events get cancelled. A key person or two leaves the company. Rumors abound. There is a sudden change in the operating numbers and the change is not positive. Your company is in the press. There is a lot of talk around the water cooler. People get together after work to have a drink (or several) and to talk about what is going on. People are concerned. You are concerned.

Fear
Fear is the first tremble caused by the winds of change. It is all about, "What is going to happen to me?" It is a quick decision that only bad can come from change. It comes from the reality that some things (and some of them possibly very important) could be lost, such as:

- "I am only a year away from vesting."

- "I have had cancer and will not be able to get life or medical insurance."

Designated *for Success*

- "Nobody will want to hire me; I am too old."

- "I will never be able to match what I make here."

- "This is my family."

- "My skills are specific to the job I have here. This job is not needed elsewhere."

- "I am in financial trouble already. I cannot afford to miss even one paycheck."

- "Here we go again. Job number nine down the tubes."

- "There are no other great jobs in Fargo."

- "I love what I do and where I live and who I work with and everything about this job."

All are real fears. All of the above can shake you up.

You are not alone. When CEOs get fired, they fear the process. They may have different fears, but they fear the unknown. We all do.

Preliminary Acceptance
If you can get through the fear stage, you will come to a point of preliminary acceptance. Once you have heard enough rumors or have gotten a wink from your boss, you will begin to accept that change is coming. It is inevitable. It is out of your control. It is on its way to you. Like it or not, you accept the probability that you will lose your job.

Mourning
When I finally accepted that I would probably lose my job of 27 years, I went to my basement and stared at the walls for a whole weekend. I felt like I had been handed divorce papers, yet was still deeply in love. I felt like a friend or relative had died. I mourned the loss. It felt like a funeral. It was one of the lowest moments of my life. Even worse, as an officer of the company, I needed to be upbeat and positive at work. I could not even roll around in my pain and suffering. Thank God for my wife. She understood and did all she could to help me through the process. And thank God for God. He helped me through, as well.

Waiting

The waiting was probably the worst part. Everything went into slow motion. Just as the rumors got more and more specific, they would change . . . things would go on hold. At one point, an agreement was reached to actually sell the part of the company that I was in. That did not end the waiting. That made it worse.

Once our part of the company was sold, we were all put on hold. We were told not to travel, not to start projects, and not to finish projects. Our old employer could not talk to us during the due diligence. The new owner did not want to talk to us (plenty of time for that later on . . . if it needed any of us). Some of our team quit. Some of our team transferred out to some safe haven in the old company. One advance scout made it onto the new team (for transition purposes . . . actually because he was clearly an outstanding person under any set of circumstances). The rest of us sat around and looked at one another.

I remember this as one of the worst times of my life. My secretary and I would literally fight over who got to read *The Wall Street Journal* first. By nine o'clock there was nothing to do. You could not run off and play golf. The new company people might call.

Everyone was so depressed that they did not really want to talk. I learned to sit and stare. After about a week of that nonsense, I learned to protect myself. I started the process of getting a new job, rather than waiting around to be handed the crumbs from our conquering heroes. I hated waiting.

Hope

There are always rumors that give you some hope. The same people that start the partially true rumors of change, start the not-one-bit-true rumors of hope. Such as:

- ■ "They have decided to close the West Coast offices. We should be fine."

- ■ "Keep it quiet, but they have decided to move the home office from Chicago to right here in Boca Raton. Boy, I would hate to be one of those fancy home office types."

- ■ "The company that is buying us has agreed to keep everyone. In fact, since its people are paid much more than ours, we will all be getting pay adjustments to bring us up to their level."

Designated *for Success*

- "I just got a peek at the new company's benefit package. Wow! It will be a major upgrade for us."

- "They have decided they really do need two chief financial officers."

- "I hear the deal fell through and our company has had a change of heart. Everything is back to normal."

- "I got the word. I cannot say who told me. We will be just fine. It is the old guys that are going out the door feet first. It is about time."

- "Word has it that all decisions will be based on seniority. With 27 years in, I will be okay."

Just when you thought things were totally lost, hope springs eternal. There is always hope.

Hope Dashed
There is always hope, until it is squashed flatter than a bug at a barn dance. Hope dashed usually shows up as:

1. The newspaper.

2. A hastily called meeting in the auditorium.

3. A news release.

4. An "Agreement in Principle" has been signed.

5. A pink slip.

In other words, hope dashed is truth. It is real. It is no longer a rumor. You have something to read or words to listen to that contain the actual facts. Most hope is followed by hope dashed. Sorry to say.

Fear Realized
You get canned. Sometimes they call it "laid off." Do not believe that one. You are not going to be getting a call anytime soon asking you back. You are fired.

The unkindest cut is the "you have been given notice." You have to stick around for a while. Sometimes there is a stay bonus if you stick around until the bitter end. Sometimes it is just, "Your services are no longer needed effective yearend." Either way, you are fired.

Deer in the Headlights

This stage of the process is basically paralysis. It is different from denial, because denial requires actual thought to occur. Deer in the headlights is exactly as it sounds. You are so overwhelmed by the emotion of the situation that you do nothing. In fact, it is a form of depression. You find it hard to get out of bed. Hard to actually go down to the state office and sign up for unemployment. People can see it in your eyes. They look like two ball bearings rolling around in a pie tin. You are stunned. Sound familiar? It can happen to any of us and to all of us. It is part of the process.

Denial

Denial is another stage you can actually spot from the outside. I had a lady in denial in my office the other day. Her company was going down the tubes fast. There was no stopping the spiral. She knew it. But she denied it.

How do I know she denied it? She told me about 10 stories of possible good outcomes for her company. She told me all the things she was trying to do to save the firm. She spent long minutes telling me about how she was working to save the jobs of her employees. Her eyes darted around frantically trying to think up new possibilities to get her and hers out of the situation.

I asked her a question. "Do you honestly think the company has an 80 percent chance of making it?" "No," was her answer. "Then show me your résumé." I said. "I do not have one," she replied. Classic denial.

The problem with denial is that it is based on hope, not reality. It stops you from going into the marketplace while there are still jobs to be had. It disadvantages you. It is no longer disloyal to be looking for a job when your current one is about to crater. And, as hard as it is to imagine, these situations are no longer in your control. Protect yourself.

Anger

I have yet to meet the person who did not experience anger when he or she was fired. I did. I got angry as hell. In fact, I went home, tapped on a wall to make sure I could find a hollow spot, and put my fist through the drywall. It cost about $100 to fix. But it was well worth it.

Designated *for Success*

We all get angry. It is not fair. We were not treated right. I know some people who were actually fired by e-mail. Others came in one morning to find their stuff in boxes on the loading dock. It is a lousy, degrading, demeaning, discouraging, anger-inducing part of life. I hate it.

It is not important that you get angry. It is very important how you handle that anger. You have options. You can:

- ■ **Turn your back on the person firing you** and not listen to anything past "I'm sorry to be letting you go." **There is money to be had during the firing process. Listen very carefully to your options and rights.** Save your anger for later.

- ■ **Blow up at the person firing you.** I have had to fire dozens of good people during my decades in business. I do not feel any better about it than the person being fired. I would like to be of as much comfort and actual help to the person being fired as possible. That predisposition to help ends quickly when the employee lashes out at me.

- ■ **Burn bridges.** Whatever industry you are in, it is a little universe. Burn a bridge today and regret it tomorrow. It is better to leave under the best of circumstances, not the worst.

- ■ **Sabotage the workplace.** Screw up the computers. Delete and throw away important files. Leave things in shambles. Another form of burning bridges. And if you do it in such a way that the company can never tie it back to you, you are just plain gutless. Leave with your ethics and dignity intact. Tempting as sabotage might sound, it is better to just leave.

- ■ **Stay angry for life.** I am amazed at how many people choose to carry this baggage with them forever. I talk to people all the time who describe their firing with something close to rage. Often, I find that the firing occurred 10 years ago. Let it go. It does you no good. Get angry. Channel it somewhere, deal with it, and move on down the road.

You hear the stories of people coming back into the office after being fired and killing people. You hear about people getting fired and committing suicide. Letting your emotions get out of check at a time like a firing is dangerous, dangerous business. Some thoughts:

1. Get some professional help to deal with your anger. You probably still have employee assistance benefits. Use them. Cost your old company a few bucks.

2. Talk to your loved ones. Tell them about your anger. Ask them to help you through this difficult passage. You will be surprised with their willingness to help.

   If you have no one to help you, track me down. I will help you. I have been through this process and I can help. My contact information is in the back of the book.

3. Be really careful driving. I have learned from hard experience that we are distracted when we are angry. Results: speeding tickets and accidents. Be careful out there.

4. Do not make big decisions about your personal life while you are angry. This is a bad time to consider a divorce. A bad time to sell the house. A bad time to buy a fancy car. A really bad time to be in a casino. Wait until the anger is gone. Then make a rational decision.

5. Get some exercise. I run when I am angry. If I normally run two miles, I may step it up to six. It helps relieve the stress and the anger. It is good for your body and your mind.

6. Spend a little time plotting how you can move to a competitor and prove your old company wrong. Maybe the old company will not notice and really does not care. That is unimportant. It will feel like righteous activity.

7. Avoid alcohol and drugs. They may make things better for a short while. But they will make things worse in the long run. This is a bad time to be drinking.

8. If you are religious, this is a great time to get in touch with your faith and the clergy. Get all the help you can get.

9. Use outplacement services if they are offered. They know how to spot anger and how to help you deal with it.

10. Get over it. Anger is a heavy load to carry with you for life.

People like me, we can smell anger on you. We ask you questions during interviews to see if you have put the anger behind you. Such as:

Designated *for Success*

- "How did they treat you when you got fired?"

- "What did you learn from the experience?"

- "You spent 25 years there. Were you disloyal to them? Didn't your tenure mean anything?"

Pretty unfair bear baiting, I will admit. But I want to know if you are still angry. If you are a little angry, no problem. If you are still really angry, big problem. I do not hire angry people. Most people do not.

The whole point here is that the firing process triggers emotion and anger in all of us. Work your way through this stage as quickly as possible. The anger will do you no good. It will not even make you feel better.

Acceptance
And, finally, at long last, most of us come to accept our fate. We have been fired. The job is not coming back. We are not wanted here anymore. It is time to get on with our lives. It is time to get a new job.

Panic
Now that we know we need a new job, some of us panic. We have no idea how to go about getting a new job. We start to make bad decisions, such as:

- "I will never get as good a job again."

- "I would accept half my old pay if I could land a job tomorrow."

- "I have no real skills for the real world."

- "I give up."

- "I will retire early. The $450,000 I have saved up and the $1,200 a month retirement payment I can tap into at age 55 should be plenty to see me through. And I have Social Security to look forward to in just 10 short years."

- "I am too old to start over. I will downsize, move to someplace cheap, and never buy a new suit as long as I live." (You will see this guy 30 years later at someone's funeral and you will know exactly what I mean.)

A few minutes of panic can cause you to make decisions that can affect the rest of your life. Stay calm.

Everything's

Going to

Be

O.K.

EGBOK!

Game Plan

Once the anger is gone and the panic subsides, you can move into a really positive place. You can start to build a game plan for getting on with your life. First step: Take this opportunity to reconnect with your dreams.

It is entirely possible that your old job was really a dead end. It may have been nothing like the dream job you desired when you first started out. What was that dream? Spend some time reconnecting.

Next step. Get some help. I mentioned outplacement. Outplacement is often offered to those who are fired. It is a healthy step in finding new employment. These professionals help you set up a productive game plan, including working up a résumé and building up a network. They provide some discipline for the process. I am completely positive about outplacement.

If you don't have outplacement available to you, follow this plan:

1. Get your résumé together.

2. Write a detailed description of each job held written down in an orderly manner.

3. Write out your salary progression and your most recent compensation package. Think through your ideal compensation package at your next job.

4. Write out your contact list—your network. Do this in such a way that you can keep track of who you called, what you learned, and when you should

call them back. If you do not have 100 people on your contact list, you are not trying very hard.

5. Read the book *Rites of Passage at $100,000 to $1 Million+* by John Lucht.

   The book is full of useful resources that will help you in your situation.

6. Ask someone to help you stay positive and confident. Pick someone who is positive and confident. Pick someone who has a job. Contact him or her as needed to get you through the day. I see a lot of good people lose their positive attitude and confidence as they work their game plan and do not get early results.

   If you have no one to contact, contact me. I will help you.

7. Use the Internet to find jobs. Use newspapers to find jobs. Look for firms moving to your area. Look for firms that are expanding. Contact your old competitors. Think through your skills and dreams and consider what jobs outside your old industry might fill the bill.

8. Be absolutely straight with any executive recruiter (headhunter) that contacts you. You may have to document facts later in the process. Do not exercise an executive recruiter unless you are serious about the job he or she is seeking to fill. You do not want to build up a bad reputation with these important resources. I know for a fact that they have long memories (and good records of your previous contacts with them).

9. *Do not stop looking just because you think you have a job offer locked up.*

   Things can fall through at the last moment. Better offers may be out there. This is a really easy mistake to make. It can break your heart.

10. Rule of thumb: interviewing processes that go on and on . . . do not result in jobs. Don't fall for the sucker punch.

11. *Never lose sight of the fact that you are a valuable human being. You matter. You matter to your family. You matter to society. You matter to your neighbors. You still matter to your industry. You matter to me. You matter to God. You are a valuable human being, whether you find a job in one week or in two years. You matter.*

Work the Game Plan

A quick word about working the game plan. The game plan is very hard to work while you are on that two month tour of Australia. If you need a break from all of the stress and strain, take one. Take one like you would if you had a job. Take a week or two. The sooner you get after the new job, the better. And, these game plans do not work themselves. You have to get behind the steering wheel and steer the car. It is your game plan, not the outplacement service's game plan. Work it like a job. If you find your golf handicap dropping during this process, you are not with the program. Work the game plan.

Success

Success is landing the new gig. Before you declare victory, here are some thoughts.

First thought, while negotiating for the job, remember my good advice: **If you do not ask, you do not get.** Ask for more salary. Ask for the perks that come with the job. Ask for at least three weeks' vacation. Ask. If you do not ask, you do not get.

I actually believe the following: **If you do not ask for too much, you have not asked for enough.** If you do not make them sputter and say things like, "That is more than I make," then you are not negotiating hard enough. Be willing to embarrass yourself. The embarrassment passes quickly and you may, in that time, find the top of what they are willing to pay you.

Title can be important. Ask what the proposed title means. Are there perks or privileges that go with such a title? What are those same perks and privileges for the next title up the line? Do not be shy to ask about title. Title often means something.

You do not have to jump at the first offer that comes your way. There is more than one job out there for you. If the offer suits you, cool, take the job. If it is short of what you really want, go slow. This is a poor time to start settling.

Get it in writing. If you are getting a legitimate offer, it should be in writing. And you may want to consider the offer overnight. You do not have to lunge at it right then and there.

Once you get the job, thank people. Thank your network. Let them know you landed. Thank the executive recruiters that worked with you. Thank the person that kept you positive and confident. Give special thanks to anyone who really helped you. The last time I got a new job, I sent the guy who helped me some flowers. I bought him dinner the next time I saw him. I made it clear that I really appreciated his help. You never know, you may need that help again.

By the way, **congratulations.** You have just made it through one of life's difficult moments. If you made it all the way from fired to hired, you are a winner. If you are still in the process, you are a winner in waiting. Either way, you are a valuable human being. You matter. Good things are ahead.

"I'm not the smartest or most talented person in the world, but I succeed because I keep going, and going, and going."

—Sylvester Stallone

■ Chapter 24
Dealing with the Ups and Downs of Your Career

"The way I see it, if you want the rainbow, you gotta put up with the rain."

—Dolly Parton

I have been up and I have been down. All in all, I like up better. With extremely rare exception, if you have a long career, you will experience setbacks from time to time. Few of us get to go from trainee to the top of our profession without getting knocked back once, twice, or several times. Success is rarely a straight line.

"Don, do you remember how I've always told you that you are a real asset for our company? Well, we are selling the assets."

"Don, well, this is going to be a bit of an awkward conversation. We want to make a change and it is time for you to take a step back."

Both of the above statements have come my way during the past decade. In both cases, my job changed quickly. In both cases, my greatest success was still out in front of me.

There is that old saying out there that it is not so much what happens to you, as what you do when it happens. When a setback comes your way, it is time to deal with it. Let us look at the topic of "dealing with it."

One of my best friends got passed over for a job early in his career. It hurt his ego so badly that he quit. He has regretted quitting to this day. His ego got in the way of his good sense.

Another friend of mine lost his job and immediately lost his confidence. He never returned to the high level of employment that he had before the job loss.

However, the examples that I enjoy the most are the ones where a setback becomes the stage for great future success. It serves to interrupt a direction that was not really headed toward achieving lifetime goals and gives the individual an opportunity to get back on a more positive track.

I just read *Tearing Down the Walls* by Monica Langley. It is about the retired CEO of Citigroup, Sandy Weill, and how he fought his way to the top of his profession. I recommend that you read the book. You will see that even Sandy Weill had his significant setbacks. The important thing is that he pretty much won everything in the end.

When setbacks come your way, they are often presented to you by your boss. A couple of things to remember, your boss does not get to choose whether or not you are going to achieve your lifetime goals. That is your choice. Secondly, the boss has a primary responsibility to look out for what is best for the company. The only person who has a primary responsibility for your career is you. So your success is up to you.

The most important advice on this subject that I can give myself or anyone else who is willing to listen is to keep your head and your wits about you when faced with a setback. Listen to your options. Listen for opportunity. Think about your alternatives. Check your ego at the door. And . . . do not accept the setback as final. There is opportunity out there to be had. A bump in the road is just that . . . a bump.

And you know what, your boss may be right. It is possible that you have been in the wrong job. That does not mean that you are a failure. It means you have been in the wrong job.

This is a time to think about getting more focused on what it is that you do really well. Perhaps you would be great in your old job, but at a different company . . . a different environment. Perhaps you would do really well capitalizing on your technical skills rather than your management skills. Change is good. New directions can be invigorating. Look for the positives and you will find them.

Designated *for Success*

Setbacks are for everyone. Did you just get demoted or passed over for a big promotion? Welcome to the club. Get over it as quickly as you can. Do not let your ego make decisions for you. Redouble your efforts to achieve everything you want in life. Setbacks are for everyone. **Success is reserved for those who refuse to let a setback get in the way of their eventual total success.**

Stay confident. Stay positive. Keep your eye on the prize. Success is still . . . and always will be . . . out there for you to grab. Use both hands. Grab all you can.

"Sleep, riches, and health, to be truly enjoyed, must be interrupted."

—Johann Paul Friedrich Richter

Part Four—
How to Win Everything
in the End

*"There is no such thing as
expecting too much."*

—Susan Cheever

■ Chapter 25
Be Careful What You Ask For, You Might Just Get It

"Success is a journey, not a destination."

—Ben Sweetland

For years I wanted nothing more than to someday become the regional vice president of my company. The person holding that job—the guy with the great big office in the corner—who drove a company-paid-for Cadillac—who had the classiest assistant in the world—who commanded respect just by stepping into the room—who told us that he was a millionaire—was nearly a god in my eyes. I dreamed about someday becoming a "Pete Mims." (Mr. Mims was our regional vice president.)

Looking back, that was a pretty foolish goal. I had no idea what he really did for a living. I really had no idea what kind of money he made. He and I never spoke about his frustrations with the job. I had no idea if or how the job affected the rest of his life. I was basing my career goal on the barest outward trappings of one person's job.

Sometimes it is hard to envision all the success we are capable of achieving without having a role model for that success. And sometimes, when we get up close and personal with that hard-to-find role model, we learn that the job is not everything we had expected. Case in point. . . .

The first extremely successful person that I was privileged to work closely with was a gentleman by the name of Jack Callahan. Jack was the president of our division. Prior to that assignment he had held every top job a person could hold in our company, short of chairman. At one point in his long career, he had led tens of thousands of people. Jack was and is one of business's finest leaders.

What did I learn from working so closely with Jack? Enough for another book. However, in this book, I want to concentrate on the surprising things I learned from him.

He worked like a dog. When he was new in the job of running our division, people used to literally follow him into the men's room to discuss business with him. He would often have early morning breakfast meetings. He would often have dinner meetings. He frequently attended things like Board meetings on the weekend. He had very little time for anything outside of work.

Jack is married to Lucy, one of the great women in the world. He has terrific children, now grown adults with interesting lives and careers. He has interests outside of work. He has a significant amount of money in his pocket. The only thing he was in short supply of was . . . the time to enjoy them all. Jack had an all-consuming job.

I learned that despite the fact that I had built Jack into nearly a fantasy figure of success, he had problems just like the rest of us human beings. He has two elbows that cause him pain and suffering (injured in a fall). He had a gall bladder that acted up and needed to be removed. (I saw him travel a few hundred miles to give an hour-long speech in front of hundreds of people just days after his surgery— absolutely amazing!) He was occasionally politically frustrated at work.

Jack suffered disappointment when all of his and our hard work went for naught due to the Hurricane Andrew. That hurricane devastated thousands of lives in Florida. It also wiped out our company earnings for the year. It turned a great year into a horrible year. It changed the ending on a turnaround story from "mission accomplished" to "wait until next year." A huge disappointment.

I saw Jack weep when friends suffered or died. I watched him deal with professional disappointment. His life was not perfect. I had foolishly expected it would be.

Designated *for Success*

All that said, Jack's career is and was, by anyone's standards, hugely successful. Jack is a fulfilled man today and seems comfortable with his success. But all that success came at a price. Are you willing to pay that price?

I mentioned Pete Mims earlier. Looking back, I wanted his job and never even knew what that job paid. Imagine working 20 years to try to get that job and not really knowing what that job paid. Imagine not really knowing the price one has to pay to get that job or do that job. ***Do you know the price of your dream?***

Be careful what you ask for, you might just get it. Understand what you are getting into. I have one of my favorite employees who tells me that she wants my job, but has no intention of doing my job the way I do it . . . moving, traveling so much, working the hard pile, and such. Oh really! Good luck. Maybe you can pull it off. More likely, you cannot.

There is a price to pay in making your dream come true. The stiffer the price, the bigger the achievement. What price are you willing to pay? Think it through.

Too often, unrealistic career goals back a person into a very narrow window of opportunity and he or she ends up frustrated by lack of success. For example, people want to be chairman, but they are unwilling to move to the worldwide headquarters when that day arrives. They figure that they will either wear out the corporate jet commuting or they will move the 5,000-person headquarters down the street from their house. Is it possible? Yes. Is it likely? Not even close.

Do not work 30 or 40 years in one direction without thinking through the end game. I submit that you will get what you work and ask for. ***You will be ultimately successful*** in your game plan. Just make sure that your game plan includes happiness. Because, at the end of the day, you have not really achieved your goals if you end up miserable. Life is a balance. Do not forget the "your happiness" part of the balance.

I met the Dalai Lama recently. After meeting him, I was curious to learn more about his Buddhist beliefs. I read a book about the Dalai Lama. In that book, he stated that the purpose of life is to be happy. I know very little else about the Dalai Lama or Buddhism. This much I do know, they have the "be happy" part just about right.

Winning without happiness is probably not winning.

"The U.S. Constitution doesn't guarantee happiness, only the pursuit of it. You have to catch up with it yourself."

—Benjamin Franklin

■ Chapter 26
You Win When You Say You Win

"Success has always been easy to measure. It is the distance between one's origins and one's final achievement."

—Michael Korda

I have spent a lot of your reading time discussing Olympic-size dreams. I am obviously a big believer in achieving everything you can imagine. The U.S. Army has it right:

Be all that you can be.

However, there comes a time when everyone needs to reflect on how much progress he or she has made. For most of us, that time comes as early as our 50s. For others, much later. My prayer is that every person takes that opportunity to treat himself or herself well—to reflect on his or her accomplishments and take pride in both his or her journey and achievements.

The truth is, you win when you say you win.

Did you come up a little short of being elected President of the United States? Miss out on your Oscar? Did someone else walk off with your Olympic dream? Did not make chairman? Have you given your career your best shot and taken it as far as it is going to go? Are you close to retirement and still a little short of the career goal? Most motivational people would tell you to toughen up and get back after it. I am here to say, declare victory and call it a day.

You win when you say you win. It is absolutely acceptable to fall a little short of a grand goal . . . as long as you gave it your best shot. If you are 35 years old and reading this part, turn the pages quickly. I am writing this part for you more seasoned veterans—the ones that have run the career marathon and are coming toward a successful finish. God bless you for your journey. It has been a long haul. You deserve to feel great about everything you have accomplished.

"How can they say my life is not a success? Have I not for more than sixty years got enough to eat and escaped being eaten?"

—Logan Pearsall Smith

■ Chapter 27
Do Something with Your Success

*"Caring about others, running the risk of feeling,
and leaving an impact on people, brings happiness."*

—Rabbi Harold Kushner

You know that we do stand on the shoulders of those who went before us. You did not get to where you are by your hard work alone. You had a lot of help.

And so I urge you to give something back. Like what?

An old boss of mine, Don Shanks, left his door open for anyone who wanted to come into his office to discuss his or her hopes, dreams, and careers. Anyone. Don always had time for you as an individual. He demonstrated his care for people every day of his life.

Cynthia Reddix worked with me for a long time. She partnered up with a local school and mentored kids. She provided advice, encouragement, and a positive role model for every kid with whom she worked (including this 50-something kid).

Cary Stone is a long-time friend who started a newsletter and a web site to help keep her retired friends and others in contact with one another. She refuses any financial help. She does it out of respect for her circle of friends.

Ted Silverburg is a long-time friend who teaches visually impaired children how to surf.

Jim Strohl coached young "up and comers" on how to manage and how to become a professional at your job.

Bill Walsh is a long-time colleague. He retired from his first career and is now a fishing boat captain. He takes kids with medical problems on fishing trips. He will be horrified that I even mentioned his kind act. He does it quietly and from his heart.

Jim Grayson is an executive recruiter. He travels to Poland to teach Western business techniques to Polish businessmen and women.

Bob Leibold is a retired company president. He took the first year of his retirement and devoted it to volunteering full time in his church.

Coach Bill O'Rourke has stayed in touch with me for nearly 40 years. When I need advice, he is always there for me. His high-school coaching will last throughout my life.

My college coach, Steve Simmons, went to South America and Africa to bring first-class coaching to outstanding athletes in those locales. He also has served our United States Men's Track and Field team and our Olympic team.

My long ago boss, Jack Callahan, serves his alma mater, Bryant University, as head of its Board of Trustees.

Ed Overman, Ph.D., CPCU, was president and chief executive officer of the American Institute for Chartered Property Casualty Underwriters. He continues to serve the CPCU Society and the American Institute for CPCU even though he has been retired for years. He is my hero in the world of insurance professionalism.

David Kretch was a friend who died too young. At the time of his death he was mentoring a young associate. David started giving back early in his career.

You get the idea. All of the above are winners. Most importantly, they share their winnings with others. They reinvest in society. They make something out of their success.

Designated *for Success*

Bring your leadership to others, long before you slip out the door and into that golf shirt. There is a world of people out there who could and would benefit greatly from your interest in them. If you are a high achiever, my guess is you are very focused. Please give some thought, and lots of action, toward broadening that focus to include others. They need you and you will be the better for it.

"There are two ways of spreading light: To be the candle or the mirror that reflects it."

—Edith Wharton

■ Chapter 28
Leave Something Behind

"We look into mirrors, but we only see the effects of our times on us . . . not our effects on others."

—Pearl Bailey

Dick Haayen was the chairman of Allstate Insurance. He was a great leader. He was one of the finest insurance professionals I have ever met. Dick made one mistake. He turned 65. At age 65, he was required to retire.

I visited Dick shortly before he left the company. I told him I was not sure that Allstate would ever be as successful without him as it was with him. He asked me if I still surfed. "Yes, sir," I replied. "Do me a favor," he said. "Next time you are at the beach, take a handful of water out of the ocean and throw it onto the sand. Then, take a look at the ocean and see how much it has changed. That is how much Allstate will change without me."

I have since heard a similar story in several other places. Dick was not trying to be original. He was trying to teach a young guy a lesson. As big and powerful as we are, the world will probably get along just fine when we are gone.

I did not believe Dick Haayen for a second. I thought he was being modest. He was not. Allstate is still doing well many years later. Lesson learned.

Even if I turn out to be the best executive in the history of my company, it will be "Don who?" shortly after I am gone. And, if I have done my job well, that will be absolutely acceptable.

I cringe when I think of the winners I know walking out the door on retirement day, without capturing their experience and insights before they leave. Leave something behind to help those that follow. What can you leave?

- A well-running business.

- A staff that knows as much as you knew because you cared enough to teach them well.

- A piece of software that automates what you used to do so well.

- A book on what you learned and how you learned it.

- A diverse group of people in which you invested as their mentor or coach.

- A charity that you helped form and fund.

- A scholarship that gives opportunity and hope to those less fortunate.

- A culture you helped build that will live long after you are gone.

- Processes that work perfectly.

- People whom you encouraged to be confident, honest, and hard working.

What is your legacy? If it is just to keep the truck on the road from this date to that date, that is not enough. Leave something behind. Something that adds lasting value to your industry and to society.

"Sow good services: sweet remembrances will grow from them."

—Madame de Stael

■ Chapter 29
A Word About Your Health

"*Prayer indeed is good, but while calling on the gods a man should himself lend a hand.*"

—Hippocrates

Every now and then we hear on television about some rich lawyer who died without a will. We hear about the athlete who worked his way to the top and then died early from some easily curable disease. These incidents remind us of how focused we can become on the one and only thing we do. This single focus is not a good thing . . . it can kill us.

I have had the good fortune to work for companies that required me to get an annual physical. **So far, these physicals have saved my life twice.** On one occasion the exam found a potential cancer and I was able to have it removed before it became a cancer. The second save came when an actual cancer was found. Again, I was able to have the cancer removed. I wonder if I would have gotten the physicals without the company requirement. Quite honestly, I doubt it.

These two physicals saved my life.

How about you? When was the last time you had a physical—a complete physical? And, by the way, what about that nagging physical or mental problem that you have been putting off your visit to a doctor because you are too busy right now? Wouldn't it devastate you to find out that it could have been easily treated if only you had come in a month earlier?

About two years ago I had a 99 percent successful physical exam. It turned out I was healthy as a horse, save the possible prostate cancer they found. More exams followed. Sure enough, I had prostate cancer. I had not one symptom—not one clue that a problem was brewing. Thank God for good doctors and the PSA test.

I was lucky. The doctors caught it in time, operated on me, and saved my life. It turns out that they did not catch it in an early stage. They caught it just before it would have become a real life-endangering problem. I am 100 percent healthy and happy today, thanks to Doctor Hoshizaki and my great surgeon, Dr. Michael Blum.

I found out I had cancer at 53 years of age. Up to that point, I was absolutely sure that I would live to be about 150 years of age. I never thought about my health. I was strong as an ox and twice as smart.

When someone tells you that you have cancer—the kind of cancer that kills people—it gets your complete attention. In fact, I learned the news on the phone. I remember my peripheral vision closing down so much it was like I was looking through a straw. My hearing went fuzzy. I had to wait for a while before I could, ever so carefully, drive home. At home, I was greeted by my very concerned wife. The two of us did not even get out of the garage before we were both hugging and crying. Cancer. I hate it.

Cancer can stop you dead in your tracks way before you reach your goals. It can stop you dead before you have any time to enjoy a well-earned retirement. It is a force that should not be taken lightly.

How about your heart? What kind of shape is it in? I am a marathoner and in pretty good shape. Still, I learned, again during a physical exam, that I had already had at least one heart attack. I was working in New York City at the time. The doctor wanted to know if I had any stress in my job. Guess what. Stress was my job.

It turns out they did more tests and found that their exam results were incorrect. I had no prior heart attack. Still, one minute I am running around New York City and the next minute I thought I was facing a career-altering health event.

What you do not know can and will kill you. I had a good friend die last week at age 38. I went to a funeral today for a guy still in his 60s. Too soon. In both cases—too soon.

Designated *for Success*

Please take care of yourself. Do you get all the medical attention you need? If not, get it. You deserve to invest in your physical and mental well-being. Quit making excuses. Quit putting everything else before your health. Quit being afraid of what they might find. Go find out how you are doing. If there is something wrong, get it fixed. ***Please take care of yourself.*** You are a very valuable human being.

Do yourself a favor. Call for an annual physical appointment this week. At least set the appointment. That will put you into an action mode, instead of a waiting mode. Imagine that a few days' time could save your life. It happens all of the time. Do it.

Oh, and how about getting back into shape? Don't you deserve to be in the best shape possible? Let us get those excuses out in the open:

- "I am too busy to work out."

- "I do not know what to do."

- "My knees are shot and the doctor told me not to work out." (Suspicion: You were not listening correctly. The doctor probably did not say "do not exercise." The doctor may have said "quit running.")

- "I am big boned and can easily carry the 350 pounds I weigh."

- "I am too tired" (my current excuse).

- "I get home too late."

- "I have kids at home."

- "I travel too much."

- "It interferes with my smoking and drinking."

- "I get plenty of exercise in my garden."

- "I will start working out again when I retire."

- "I hate to sweat."

- "It is too hot out."

- "It is too cold out."

- ■ "I look horrible in running clothes."

- ■ "Running is boring."

Most of us have a favorite excuse. The truth is, it is just too much like real work. The truth is, we think we can get away with it. Well, I know I cannot. If I take off a month or so, I have to get into my suits with a shoehorn. I feel sluggish. I look worse than normal. I am not a happy camper.

You deserve to keep yourself at peak efficiency whether you are 20 something or "older than hell" something.

And one last health rant—about that drinking and/or smoking. Just when are you going to give that up? Drinking and smoking will not serve you well in the long run. That is my opinion. Just cough three times if you disagree.

"They say such nice things about people at their funerals that it makes me sad that I'm going to miss mine by just a few days."

—Garrison Keillor

■ Chapter 30
A Word About Your Money

"*Mommy, we're not going to be poor again, are we?*"

"*Not as long as you have that rare blood type.*"

—Brett Butler

Your money deserves your serious, and early, attention. The power of investing money wisely over time is absolutely awesome. And, guess what? You are going to need that money someday. Trust me.

Retirement sneaks up on you. If you are prepared, it is likely to be a sweet time of life. If you arrive at your retirement party unprepared, start working out your plans to shrink your life down to size. Think public transportation and government cheese.

Jack Callahan explained the financial life cycle to me. It goes like this . . .

- ■ In the beginning you are dirt poor.

- ■ Eventually you earn enough to buy or rent the basics of life—food, clothing, and shelter.

- ■ Then you start to make good money and you can upgrade to some higher quality stuff.

- ■ Then the kids go to college and you go into to debt.

- After the kids are out of college, you pay your way out of debt and start to save.

- Once you are debt-free you can put away a nice nest egg.

- Then you retire and pray that you do not outlive your money.

So far, that is exactly how it has worked for me. And the closer I get to retirement, the closer I observe what happens to those who do not save their money throughout their working life. They:

- Move to places you would not voluntarily visit.

- Downsize their house . . . then downsize their condominium . . . then downsize their apartment . . . then downsize their mobile home . . . then move in with relatives.

- Quit doing anything that costs money.

- Spend a lot of time looking for coupons.

- Buy cheap stuff in bulk.

- Quit traveling.

- Never pick up a check.

- Do not call.

- Sweat out summer with the air conditioning off.

- Start to bitch about the government and the economy.

- Talk bad about the rich people (anyone making more than $25,000 a year).

- Learn to work the return policy and the insurance claim.

- Are suckers for get-rich-quick schemes.

- Work jobs earning one-tenth of what they used to make.

- Are pretty much financially miserable.

Now, was that just a tirade about poor people? Absolutely not. I have respect for people that goes far beyond their economic means. I am talking about good people who earned good money and said goodbye to it before it ever saw the inside of a 401(K) plan. I am talking about people who retire too soon or live too long or save too little. Working long and hard and ending up broke—it is just not right.

Retirement planning is serious business. It deserves your attention right now, no matter what your age. Get a financial counselor and get a plan in place. Spread the risk. Invest in sensible things. Put the money away and never touch it. Turns out that you will need plenty of it starting right after the retirement party.

A good CEO puts something away for future contingencies. As CEO of your career, you need to plan carefully for whatever might come your way in the future. Again, if you do not do it, who will?

"Another good thing about being poor is that when you are seventy your children will not have you declared legally insane in order to gain control of your estate."

—Woody Allen

Designated *for Success*

■ Chapter 31
A Word About Retirement

"Why not learn to enjoy the little things . . . there are so many of them."

—Anonymous

I have a friend named John Fowler. Actually, John just died this past week. I was fortunate enough to speak to him a day or so before he passed. John had a great life.

When he retired from a very successful business career, he decided to do everything he ever dreamed of doing. I am not sure I have all of these right or in the right order, but he:

■ Became a cross-country truck driver (I heard that lasted one-half of one trip).

■ Worked in the stands at Angels baseball games.

■ Worked at a golf course.

■ Delivered the mail.

He did not need the money. He just wanted to give these new professions a try. John is my hero. I am thankful he got a chance to do it all before the final curtain call.

I have had everything a person can have in life. I have been poor and wealthy. Healthy and sick. Low man in the office and CEO. A father. A husband. President of a charity. An executive officer in an industry society. An All-American. A member of an athletic Hall of Fame and more. The one thing I have never had is my freedom. I am not anxious to get it, but when, please God, the day arrives, I want to do it like John Fowler. There is more to life than just working for an insurance company—or any kind of company.

I plan to have a writing and speaking career when I retire. I do not know how long that will last, but I will give it a good shot. Past that, I have got other stuff I want to try.

Do you have any plans for your retirement? I ask you that because I am pretty sure that just keeping busy is not enough to keep you happy. Give it some thought. Develop some outside interests well before the retirement party. You might as well enjoy the paid vacation you will earn at the end of your working career. In fact, you may want to save some of your lifetime goals for the retirement years.

I have always thought of retirement as going on summer vacation for the rest of your life. I love what I am doing now. I am sure I will love my summer vacation, as well.

A good CEO thinks through the end game. You are the CEO of your whole career, including the cool part that comes after you retire.

"He is rich that is satisfied."

—Thomas Fuller

Designated *for Success*

■ Chapter 32
Thank Somebody

"Example moves the world more than doctrine."

—Henry Miller

One of the greatest joys I have had in my life is the opportunity to thank those who have made my life better. I try my best to thank them personally and publicly. Here is an incomplete list of those who have really helped me to become the man I am today, a happy man who is still very much a work in progress:

- ■ Eric Thorson, thank you for teaching me the basics of the business.

- ■ Jack Lamm, thank you for making me read the manual.

- ■ Jack Jones, thank you for teaching me to see the humor at work.

- ■ To the ladies I first supervised, Elaine Jaco, Sally Kotnik, Jean Hein, and Clair Duval, thank you for letting an amateur practice my supervisory skills.

- ■ Bill Smith, thanks for recognizing my shortcomings and giving me the tools to deal with them.

- ■ Don Shanks, thanks for keeping your door open to me throughout my life. You are one of the finest leaders I could ever try to model.

- Jim Strohl, thanks for taking a chance on me. Thanks for making me know my profession. Thanks for your encouragement and friendship.

- Judy Haddock, thanks for being difficult to manage. Sounds strange, but you taught me that exceptional people sometimes require exceptional attention. The extra effort I put in was worth it. You are a loyal, smart, and hardworking person and I am proud to have you as my friend. Thanks for all the hard work for all those years.

- Dad, thanks for giving me the room to grow and to gain my confidence. Thanks for planting the idea that one should never ever give up.

- Mom, thanks for always standing for my success, always.

- My sister Pam, thanks for loving me unconditionally and for your care and kindness to others.

- Pat McDonald, thanks for introducing me to the idea of being the best and showing that it was possible.

- Coach O'Rourke, thanks for teaching me to have goals in my life. Thanks also for making me work so hard to reach those goals.

- Coach Simmons, thanks for pushing beyond what I thought my limits were and teaching me what it means to be a member of a team.

- Jack Callahan, thank you for modeling "executive" for me. You taught me about empowerment and about culture change. You have my total respect forever.

- Jim Marks, thank you for helping me to see that it was possible to make my dreams come true and for your help with my errant spelling.

- Loretta Malandro and her entire staff, thank you for teaching me so much about myself and the impact that I have on others.

- To the folks at Dibianca-Berkman, thanks for teaching me about the importance of relationships and introducing me to the idea of no bad relationships.

- Dave Karp, thank you for modeling focus for me.

■ Harry Cotter, thank you for showing me what it takes to push the action. You get things done.

■ Bruce Seaman, thank you for giving me opportunities. The poem in the back *"Some of What I Do, I Do Because of You"* was written for you.

■ Cathy Buxton, thank you for increasing my social awareness while focusing strongly on the work at hand.

■ David Kahne, thank you for sharing your strategy of never leaving the studio. It works. David is a music producer and never became so corporate that he might lose his studio skills. Those skills have brought him much success. I love you David.

■ Teddi Martin, thanks for letting me practice my writing skills.

■ Ray Normann, thanks for pushing me to continue my education.

■ Bill Henderson, thanks for showing me what leadership looks like. Getting your CPCU while heading up the huge Allstate Sales team . . . an awesome achievement.

■ John Amore, thank you for helping me make my dreams come true.

■ Frank Patalano, thanks for showing me what courage looks like in the workplace. You are changing a culture. You are my hero.

■ Michael Markman, thanks for modeling succinct and straightforward messaging. I cannot even write the thank you succinctly.

■ Cynthia Reddix, thanks for being my partner as we both practiced the high-performance techniques taught to us by the folks at Malandro.

■ Ross McAdam, my eighth grade teacher, thanks for showing me that surfing could be part of a productive adult lifestyle. Glassy overhead swells to you forever.

■ Mike Fayles, Dan Fairbanks, Tom Jacobs, thanks for being my best buddies.

■ Doug Smith, thanks for teaching me that nothing good ever happens after midnight.

■ The entire Eckert family, thanks for being so important in my life.

■ Mary Fall, thank you for helping me get through some of the most exciting years of my life.

■ Robert Gorman, thanks for editing the first draft of this book. I appreciate that you paid attention during grammar classes.

■ Norm Baglini, thanks for your education and ethics leadership.

■ Larry Brandon, thanks for leading the way as a CPCU author.

■ Terrie Troxel, thanks for your continued leadership of the AICPCU.

■ To the men and women of the CPCU Society, thanks for your support and friendship over all these years.

■ Hugh McGowan, Millie Workman, Betsey Brewer, John Reynolds, Jim Nau, and Larry Klein, thanks for your CPCU leadership. My thanks also to Greg Deimling, Bill Sleeper, Ed Neff, Joe Wetter, Anita Bourke, Jim Britt, Frank Robitaille, Don Dresback, Evelyn Jackson, Mike Holm, Marsha D. Egan, Paul Felsen, Richard Lambert, Maureen McLendon, Jim Robertson, Lawton Swan . . . CPCUs all . . . for keeping me laughing and enjoying my CPCU experience for the past several decades.

■ A big "thank you" to Norma Little for her professionalism and her contagious great attitude.

■ George Hill . . . thank you for encouraging me to become a national leader in the CPCU organization and for your friendship.

■ Hugh Gaynor . . . thanks for the opportunity to manage a branch office. You built and Bob Leibold basically built a company from the ground floor up. Well done.

■ To Linda Hurzeler's parents, Bill and Alice Collins, and her brothers, Greg and Bill . . . thanks for raising Linda. She is about as good a human being as you can find on earth.

■ A big thank you to Pennington Way III for taking a chance on a guy fresh out of a 27-year career with one company. You were a great boss and you and Helen are friends forever.

I want to thank everyone who ever spent a moment teaching me. My teachers throughout the years. My coaches. My fellow workers. My bosses. My relatives and friends. My buddy Steve who taught me about overcoming adversity. Thank you all. You have made a positive difference in my life.

And I thank you for letting me write this book for you. Without someone to read it, it is a major waste of time. Thank you.

"I feel a very unusual sensation—if it is not indigestion, I think it must be gratitude."

—Benjamin Disraeli

Designated *for Success*

■ Chapter 33
Say Goodnight Gracie

"Exit, pursued by a bear."

—William Shakespeare stage direction

A word of advice. When it is your time to retire—do so. Get out of the way in an orderly, yet timely, manner. Remember the handful of seawater. They will get along somehow without you. And you—you have new things to do. Congratulations. You are a winner indeed.

"The trouble with eating Italian food is that five or six days later you're hungry again."

—George Miller

(I know the quote has nothing to do with the subject, but you have to admit it is a great quote.)

Part Five—
Words of Encouragement

In my first draft of this book, the working title was *A Winner in Waiting*. I took the title from a poem I had written that you will find in this next section. It covers the fact that I firmly believe that we are all winners or winners in waiting. I stuffed several other poems into the various chapters of the first draft. My basic thought was that they would serve to reinforce several important parts of the book and that you, the reader, might enjoy them.

A couple of things happened along the way. First, every time I mentioned the working title to someone, he or she asked me what the book was about. Next he or she would ask me what the title meant. So, it was back to the drawing boards to find a title that actually described what was inside the covers.

At about the same time, I read a book written by a friend of mine. Included in the book were several poems stuck into the various chapters . . . just like I envisioned for my book. After reading the book I realized that I had skipped over every single poem. I did not even read the first line of any of the poems. I treated them as if they were not there. That told me something about mixing poetry and business writing.

So, I still want to proffer my words of encouragement in the form of a few poems. If you are so inclined to read them, God bless you. If you chose to blow them off . . . well, welcome to the club. If you can only stand to read one poem . . . make it the first one, "A Winner in Waiting." It may be of some encouragement to you or to a friend. And if it is, it will make me feel like a winner as well.

■ A Winner in Waiting

by Donald J. Hurzeler, CPCU, CLU

Are you beaten down by life

Have you lost another race

Were you second at the finish

Has life slapped you in the face?

Is the world around you saying

That you're just not good enough

That someone does it better

That you just don't have the stuff?

I've got news for you my buddy

Let me tell you what I know

I'm aware of all your talents

This defeat is but a blow.

So get up off the canvas

Don't be jealous, don't be mad

Focus once again on winning

Victory's out there to be had.

The loss comes only

When you've given up the fight

When you agree to be a loser

When you finally said "They're right."

You are a winner now in waiting

First prize will come, my friend

Work hard and you will get it

The only question's "When?"

Don't let others tell you different

They don't know you like I do

You're a winner, don't forget it

The next champion will be you!

■ Why Not You?

by Donald J. Hurzeler, CPCU, CLU

Oscar winner

Olympic champion

Nobel laureate

Billionaire

President

Author

Founder

Proud parent

Friend

Thrilled

Fulfilled

Why not you?

Why someone else

You see on TV

Or on a stage

While you sit home

Depressed or raged

Why not you?

To take one from the list

Of things that could be

Things that really do exist

Like happiness

Make a choice

Set a goal

Do the work and believe

What you believe you can achieve

It is up to you

To do

Or watch

A life to botch

Or live so large

You'll need a barge

To freight your smiles

Stacked up in piles

Why not you?

Designated *for Success*

■ The Making of a Miracle

by Donald J. Hurzeler, CPCU, CLU

Start with a goal large enough to take a lifetime to achieve

Commit yourself completely to meeting that goal

Make hard choices that give you options

Maximize your chances for success

Take risks

Experience a setback

Shake it off

Experience a failure

Get back up

Experience discouragement in all its evil forms

Ignore them

Set your sights firmly on the goal

Claw your way back

Reach a high plateau . . . danger, danger, danger

Listen to the siren of a comfortable place—danger, danger, danger

Relax, enjoy, quietly, silently, settle for partial achievement

or

Move to higher ground

This is where real success begins

Where twenty drop off and one person moves forward

Grind away

For years with all the ups and downs

Never give up

Never give up

NEVER GIVE UP

And never lose sight of the goal

It's your goal

Your life's aspiration

Progress over time

Sometimes fast

Sometimes slow

Resolve tested

Endurance tested

Patience tested

Ability tested

You . . . tested

Then comes a day you pass the test

With honors

And finally,

Finally

Success!

Designated *for Success*

See . . . I told you . . .

It's a miracle . . . a miracle **you** *made happen!*

You're the CEO of your own life

Congratulations on your success.

■ Reinventing Me

by Donald J. Hurzeler, CPCU, CLU

It is a time for renewal

I am tired

Want to rest

Would rather retire

Or vacation

But there is a long way to go

A damn long way to go

Not a time for rest

In fact, to rest would be to rust

To never realize my full potential

Do the best I can for my family

For myself

Do my best

Do my best

Not the minimum

Not what is easy

In fact, I will have to push myself

Hard

To do those things I do not want to do

Reinvent myself, if necessary

Push

Create a new and exciting vision of the future

That future is important

It is where we will live our lives

It is time to get on with it

To get it done

I can do this

Can do whatever is needed

To win

To succeed

To feel good about myself

When at last the race is run

When finally it is over

When finally I have won

I can do this

And I will.

■ Some of What I Do, I Do Because of You

by Donald J. Hurzeler, CPCU, CLU

You have made a difference in my life

Something you said

Something you taught me

Something you model

Something about you has made a difference in my life

You are a part of what I am

How about that?

Some of what I do, I do because of you.

So . . . after all the fun

When you look back on all that you have done

Son of a gun

You done . . . good!

Thanks for being a beacon

Thanks for creating light

Thanks for helping me get

At least a few things right

You have made a difference in my life.

■ References

The quotes I used in this book came from a variety of resources. First, I want to thank the individuals quoted. Second, I want to acknowledge the books where I found these quotes. They include:

- *Bartlett's Familiar Quotations* by John Bartlett, Justin Kaplan General Editor.

- *Dick Enberg's Humorous Quotes for all Occasions* by Dick Enberg with Brian and Wendy Morgan.

- *The Book of Positive Quotations* compiled and arranged by John Cook.

- *The Great Quotations* compiled by George Seldes.

- *The Most Brilliant Thoughts of All Time (In Two Lines or Less)* edited by John M. Shanahan.

- *The Women's Book of Positive Quotes* compiled and arranged by Leslie Ann Gibson.

- *Quality Service Teamwork and the Quest for Excellence* by Michael McKee.

- *The 2,548 Best Things Anyone Ever Said* selected and compiled by Robert Byrne.

- *Tearing Down the Walls* by Monica Langley.

■ A Couple of Great Resources and How to Contact Me

1. *Rites of Passage at $100,000 to $1 Million+* by John Lucht.
   This is a terrific book for anyone who is looking for a job or is thinking about changing jobs. It includes excellent Internet tools, names and addresses of recruiters, sample résumés, sample compensation written summaries, cover letters, advice, strategies . . . the whole works.

2. Malandro Communications Inc.
   I mentioned High Performance Culture in my book. The Malandro organization specializes in cultural change. It focuses on the four critical cultural elements:

   a) Commitment

   b) Accountability

   c) Partnership

   d) Practices

   You can reach the Malandro organization at:

   Malandro Communications, Inc.
   5665 North Scottsdale Road
   Building F, Suite 130
   Scottsdale, Arizona 85250
   Phone: (602) 894-1630

3. My contact information:
   Donald J. Hurzeler, CPCU, CLU
   311 Boulder Drive
   Lake in the Hills, Illinois 60156
   e-Mail: djhzz@aol.com

Designated *for Success*

■ Index